WHO SAW HIM DIE

A Play

TUDOR GATES

SAMUEL   FRENCH

LONDON
NEW YORK   TORONTO   SYDNEY   HOLLYWOOD

© 1975 BY TUDOR GATES

This play is fully protected under the copyright laws of the British Commonwealth of Nations, the United States of America, and all countries of the Berne and Universal Copyright Conventions.

All rights are strictly reserved.

It is an infringement of the copyright to give any public performance or reading of this play either in its entirety or in the form of excerpts without the prior consent of the copyright owners. No part of this publication may be transmitted, stored in a retrieval system, or reproduced in any form or by any means, electronic, mechanical, photocopying, manuscript, typescript, recording, or otherwise, without the prior permission of the copyright owners.

SAMUEL FRENCH LTD, 26 SOUTHAMPTON STREET, STRAND, LONDON WC2E 7JE, or their authorized agents, issue licences to amateurs to give performances of this play on payment of a fee. **The fee must be paid, and the licence obtained, before a performance is given.**

Licences are issued subject to the understanding that it shall be made clear in all advertising matter that the audience will witness an amateur performance; and that the names of the authors of the plays shall be included on all announcements and on all programmes.

The royalty fee indicated below is subject to contract and subject to variation at the sole discretion of Samuel French Ltd.

The publication of this play must not be taken to imply that it is necessarily available for performance by amateurs or professionals, either in the British Isles or overseas. Amateurs intending production must, in their own interests, make application to Samuel French Ltd or their authorized agents, for consent before starting rehearsals or booking a theatre or hall.

    Basic fee for each and every
       performance by amateurs   Code L
       in the British Isles

In theatres or halls seating 600 or more the fee will be subject to negotiation.

In territories overseas the fee quoted above may not apply. Application must be made to our local authorized agents, or if there is no such agent, to Samuel French Ltd, London.

Applications to perform the play by professionals should be made to ERIC GLASS Ltd, 28 Berkeley Square, London W1X 6HD.

ISBN 0 573 01568 6

MADE AND PRINTED IN GREAT BRITAIN BY
LATIMER TREND & COMPANY LTD PLYMOUTH

MADE IN ENGLAND

WHO SAW HIM DIE?

First presented by Charles Ross in association with Arthur Talbot Rice at the Theatre Royal, Haymarket, London, on the 8th May 1974, with the following cast of characters:

Superintendent Pratt	Stratford Johns
John Rawlings	Lee Montague
Dr Adcock	Christopher Guinee
Christine	Elizabeth Wallace
Police Sergeant	Earl Robinson
Mick Jennings	Tony Parkin

The play directed by Philip Grout

Settings by John Page

ACT I
Scene 1   Dr Adcock's surgery
Scene 2   The same

ACT II
Scene 1   A flat in Willesden
Scene 2   A cellar

Time – the present

AUTHOR'S NOTE

I do hope that any repertory theatres or amateur companies thinking of presenting *Who Saw Him Die?* will not be deterred by the three sets. As a neo-realistic play, the set helps, but there is no reason why *Who Saw Him Die?* should not be performed in blacks, without scenery.

The play was originally envisaged for the stage of the Mercury Theatre in London, where another play of mine was being performed. The Mercury has a tiny, raked stage with a short flight of wooden steps leading up to a door on the back wall (which leads to the only dressing room). Thus was the cellar scene invented and I wrote the play backwards, from there.

In fact, *Who Saw Him Die?* (then entitled *Who Killed Jack Robin?*) was tried out at Surrey's lovely Richmond Theatre, where we had a rather surrealist set, with just a pair of hung window-arches, for example, suggesting Jack's hide-out. There was no Act Two, Scene one cupboard in that production but, again, this does not need to be heavily carpentered; it can be suggested.

The original programme required a certain amount of attention to detail. Calling Jack Robin by his name obviously gave away the plot, which is why I wrote in the lines about Johnny Rawlings. When we played at the Theatre Royal, Haymarket, we decided to list even the characters who are only heard off-stage, since so many inferences can be drawn by audiences from the names listed in the programme. Will Mick Jennings return, or will he not? If unlisted, he obviously won't.

A pity one cannot include a programme note for the body, which is an extremely arduous and unrewarding role (except perhaps for the gasp he always gets). There is no reason of course why he shouldn't take a curtain call at the end, grisly make-up and all. It always seemed a bit unfair to me that Jack invariably got the credit for the part when he was in his dressing-room doing the crossword.

But that's show business.

T.G.

ACT I

SCENE 1

The houselights fade and, as the audience ceases to chatter, the sound of a news broadcast is heard. When the CURTAIN *rises, the broadcast is faded out*

Announcer BBC Radio Four. Here are the news headlines. A dock strike now seems imminent following the joint announcement by the Port of London Authority and the Transport and General Workers' Union that their talks have broken down . . . British European Airways have revealed that metal fatigue was the cause of the Viscount crash just outside Brussels in April . . . The police investigation into a missing man, a former Superintendent at Scotland Yard, took a new turn today following the discovery . . .

The CURTAIN *rises on a room in the surgery of Dr Adcock. It is not the main consulting room, but one just off it, used for examinations or as a changing-room. There is an orthopaedic couch in the centre of the room, running up and down stage. On the couch lies a body covered by a sheet. The sheet is partly bloodstained, particularly in the area covering the face. The rear wall is a frosted glass partition, and from time to time we can see the indistinct figures of three people who remain in the background of the room throughout the scene*

As the CURTAIN *rises Dr Adcock is adjusting the sheet over the body's face. He goes to wash his hands. A car door slams and the engine is cut out. Dr Adcock dries his hands on a paper towel and goes out behind the screen, as the Sergeant's shadow crosses the screen and a doorbell rings. The Sergeant, behind the screen, goes to answer the bell*

Sergeant This way, please, Superintendent Pratt.

Immediately there is a noisy scene behind the frosted glass screen. The figure of Christine moves towards Pratt but is blocked by the figure of the Sergeant. The figure of another man, Jennings, rises from a chair and also approaches Pratt, but from a different angle. The following dialogue is all delivered off, behind the screen

Christine You! I thought you'd come. You bastard!
Pratt Keep her out of my way, Sergeant, until I want her.
Adcock Look after her, Sergeant!
Sergeant Yes, sir. Come on now, Miss.

As the Sergeant gently eases Christine upstage their figures, behind the screen become less distinct. Christine is sobbing

Jennings Do we have to hang around here?
Pratt Yes.

Pratt enters from the screen, followed by Adcock. The whole opening section is played with complete fluidity, so that when Pratt now enters the surgery it is all part of one continuous movement, which loses its impetus only as Pratt halts immediately at the sight of the body. Dr Adcock, who stands behind Pratt, is in his late thirties, of average height and build. He looks like a doctor. Pratt does not quite look like anything. He has not the bearing one would expect from a man in his position (he is a Superintendent of Police), because he tends to stoop. All the vigour with which he entered visibly deflates as he looks across at the body, like an actor who has walked on in the wrong scene. Pratt transfers his disbelieving stare to Adcock. His words are almost a petulant accusation

Pratt Oh, no!
Adcock Did you know him?
Pratt (*disappointed*) Yes, I know him—knew him.
Adcock (*politely*) I'm sorry. (*He walks past Pratt to his desk*)

Pratt moves to the body, picks up the corner of the sheet so that he can look down on the face of the corpse. Adcock looks across to him. Pratt screws up his face in disgust at the sight

Pratt Ugh. (*He replaces the sheet*) What a mess.
Adcock The driving mirror went through his head.

Pratt's voice is accusing, suspicious, as he thumbs towards the room behind the screen

Pratt How'd they get away so lightly then?
Adcock Because the driver was wearing a safety belt and because the woman was in the back seat.
Pratt Oh. (*He clears his throat*) I see. (*He circles the corpse, staring down at it*) Right then . . .
Adcock And it's not quite true to say they got off lightly. Both suffered cuts and bruises and the woman, in particular, is in a state of shock.
Pratt (*staring down at the corpse*) Yes—yes.
Adcock (*brusquely*) And I'd like to get them both to hospital for a check-up, as quickly as possible.
Pratt Yes. I'd like to ask a few questions.
Adcock (*with reluctance*) Well, all right. But I must see to these people. And I have a lot of work to get through.
Pratt You carry on. The public like their pound of flesh, don't they.

Adcock looks across at him, surprised

Adcock Uh?
Pratt Doctors, policemen. They expect us to work all hours.

Adcock Oh. Yes.

Pratt You didn't see it, did you?

Adcock The accident? No. I heard it. It was just across the road. Apparently the car hit the wall on the corner, head on. It's not the first accident there's been there and it won't be the last.

Pratt Yes. Then what?

Adcock I dashed out to see what had happened. Asked someone to call emergency. Had them brought over here. There was nothing I could do for this one.

Pratt (*gloomily*) Mmm.

Pratt stares down at the body, rubbing his chin thoughtfully. Adcock looks across at him

Adcock (*after a pause*) Are you all right?

Pratt wakes out of a reverie

Pratt What?

Adcock You seem—depressed.

Pratt (*with some interest*) Do I? I get moods of depression. It's the job, I think. Doctors have nothing for it, have they? Except pills.

Adcock (*disconcerted*) I—er—it's a specialist matter.

Pratt Really? I find it very common.

Adcock I mean, I'm not a psychiatrist.

Pratt Neither am I. But I get it just the same. (*He demonstrates*) It's like my head is splitting in half.

Adcock (*after a brief pause*) Yes. Er—Superintendent—I really must—er . . .

Adcock gestures to the screen to remind us of the woman behind, whom we can still hear from time to time, faintly sobbing

Pratt I'd just like to get the rest of your story, sir.

Adcock There's really no more to say. I had the body brought in here out of the way—and tended the others while I was waiting for the ambulance.

Pratt Yes.

Adcock The police arrived first and then—well suddenly all the excitement broke out.

Pratt Excitement?

Adcock (*irritably*) Superintendent, please don't try and pretend this is an ordinary accident case. The county police may be efficient but one doesn't get a half dozen patrol cars arriving on the scene of a straightforward car crash. Now I think I've been very patient, I haven't asked any questions . . .

Pratt (*interrupting*) That's all right, sir. You can leave all that to me.

Adcock What?

Pratt I'll ask the questions.

Pratt starts another walk around the corpse

Adcock Now look here. I have a certain duty. I am a doctor . . .

Pratt (*with a surprising strength*) And I am a policeman, sir. And we all
have our duties, unpleasant though they may sometimes be.

*Pratt stares hard at Adcock, who suddenly weakens, gives way, sits at his
desk. Pratt continues his tour of the corpse*

But you're quite right, this is no ordinary case. I will explain to you
shortly. But I must ask some more questions first.

Adcock You realize I had to send the ambulance back? I mean, damn it,
we're short enough of them, I couldn't keep it hanging about.

Pratt Quite right, sir. But I didn't keep you waiting. I wasn't far away.

Adcock That woman should have been taken to the hospital.

Pratt Yes. Tell me about the woman. Just cuts and bruises, eh?

Adcock And mild concussion. But it's the shock aspect I——

Pratt (*interrupting*) Yes. I understand. (*He gestures towards the screen*)
Who came round first? Her, or the man?

Adcock The driver.

Pratt What did he say?

Adcock Nothing much. Asked me to call his wife, I think.

Pratt You think?

Adcock Well, he did.

Pratt What's his name?

Adcock Jennings. I told all this to the Sergeant.

Pratt Tell me, sir. Please.

Adcock That's all.

Pratt That's all you know about him? His name?

Adcock That and the fact that he's the chauffeur of a hired car, taking a
couple to London for the night out. It's not my job to be a detective.

Pratt Quite right, sir. You leave that part of it to me. Did he identify the
others?

Adcock I think he said the car was booked by a Mr Christopher.

Pratt looks sharply and reprovingly at Adcock for the use of the word "think"

He did say Mr Christopher.

Pratt Right.

Adcock He didn't seem to know them otherwise.

Pratt Good. Now, what about Christine?

Adcock Christine?

Pratt (*opening the door so that Christine will hear*) That Scottish whore out
there.

Christine (*outside*) Bloody liar!

Sergeant (*outside*) Madam, calm down, please.

Pratt (*shutting the door*) What did she say when she came round?

Adcock She just kept calling out her husband's name.

Pratt What name?

Adcock Jack.

Pratt You're sure?

Adcock Of what?

Pratt Of the name?

Adcock Yes.

Pratt How did you know she's got a husband called Jack? I mean, it might not have been her husband she was calling for. Perhaps she's got a son?

Adcock I suppose that's possible.

Pratt Anything's possible. I had an aunt called Jack once.

Adcock What?

Pratt Her name was Jacqueline. We called her Jack. I mean, theoretically it's possible she was calling for my aunt. Although that's unlikely since she's been dead for many years and I doubt whether they ever met. But you see what I mean?

Adcock No, I'm afraid I don't. Your use of semantics bewilders me.

Pratt I beg your pardon?

Adcock What?

Pratt I don't know that word.

Adcock The meanings of words. Twisting them.

Pratt Semantics?

Adcock Yes.

Pratt Thank you. What were you saying?

Adcock Merely that she called out a man's name. I assumed the name to be that of the man in the car. I assumed that man to be her husband. Now I'm quite sure that it could have been your aunt . . .

Pratt It's not a joking matter, sir.

Adcock It's not to me, either. And nor to that woman.

Pratt Certainly not. Her husband is dead. Does she know?

Adcock Yes. And there's no doubt in my mind that it was her husband she was weeping for.

Pratt Good. When did you tell her?

Adcock As soon as I judged she was in a reasonably receptive state. After I'd calmed her down, given her a sedative. I don't believe in holding these things back and . . .

Pratt No, quite. Yes?

Adcock What?

Pratt What did she say?

Adcock She just—wept.

Pratt Didn't say his name? Jack?

Adcock I believe she did.

Pratt looks at him

Yes. She did.

Pratt I think you could say that we have reasonably established that this is Jack.

Adcock moves to confront him

Adcock (*firmly*) Superintendent. I really must insist that this woman goes to hospital.

Pratt I feel a little less depressed now.

Adcock I don't want to have to complain to the Commissioner.
Pratt He gets them too. A very moody man. He takes pills. On prescription, of course. I expect you'd like to call that ambulance now?
Adcock Yes.

Adcock moves towards the telephone. Before he can pick it up, Pratt halts him

Pratt There's no need. (*As Adcock looks at him*) We'll take her in the car.
Adcock Very well. And now, I hope.
Pratt Soon.
Adcock (*firmly*) Now.
Pratt I'll see she gets full medical supervision, sir. You needn't worry. Did she make any statement to the County Police when they arrived?
Adcock I wasn't letting her make any statements.
Pratt Did she say anything?
Adcock She screamed at them. Just as she did at you. Called them bastards. If you call that making a statement.
Pratt (*after a pause*) It's a matter of semantics, isn't it. (*Briskly*) Right, sir, That's all.
Adcock Thank you. You'll take them both to hospital?
Pratt Yes. Sorry to have made such a mystery of all this. But I had to be sure.
Adcock Of course.
Pratt (*indicating the body*) You know who this really is?
Adcock I beg your pardon?
Pratt I said, you know who this really is?
Adcock No.
Pratt Do you know who I am?
Adcock (*with a puzzled shrug*) I was told your name . . .
Pratt Yes? (*He waits expectantly*)
Adcock Pratt. Superintendent Pratt.
Pratt That's right. Does it mean anything to you!
Adcock I'm sorry, I don't . . .
Pratt Is the name familiar?
Adcock Yes, I think it is, but . . .
Pratt Do you know the name Kurt Edelstein?
Adcock (*frowning*) I've seen it somewhere. Oh you don't mean the German sailor who strangled all those prostitutes?
Pratt That's the one. Crampton? Remember his name?
Adcock The poisoner?
Pratt The poisoner.
Adcock Yes.
Pratt Yes. Griffen?
Adcock That poor devil . . .
Pratt (*harsh*) He wasn't a poor devil, he was a child murderer, but no matter, you remember him?
Adcock Well, yes . . .
Pratt And Spencer O'Brien?

Adcock No.

Pratt The man who put the bomb in the airplane.

Adcock Ah!

Pratt Ah! And Klemson? In court just a week ago?

Adcock The armoured car robbery.

Pratt That's it. They all made the front page, didn't they, Doctor Adcock? And so did I. I caught them. Each and every one. And got them all convicted. But you wouldn't remember my name.

Adcock I'm sorry.

Adcock looks socially embarrassed and Pratt chuckles, for the first time looks like an ordinary humorous man

Pratt I'm just pointing it out, it doesn't worry me. After all, it's like going to the pictures, isn't it? The only names you remember are the stars, you never look to see who's wrote it or who the cameraman was. Not unless you're a student of the cinema. And unless you were a bit of a criminologist I wouldn't expect you to know my name.

Adcock But I do. I mean, now you remind me.

Pratt (*humorously*) That's it. It's just a matter of being reminded, isn't it? No, it doesn't bother me, I never think about it. Just as well, in my job, not to be too well known.

Adcock (*smiling*) I suppose not . . .

Pratt (*losing his smile*) But now you have been reminded, no doubt you'll remember the case which brought me most publicity.

Adcock stares at him and then, with sudden comprehension, at the body

Adcock Oh, my God—of course. Christopher . . .

Pratt That's right, doctor, I mean James Christopher, alias John Fortune, alias God knows how many names but, popularly known as Jack Robin—(*He moves to the top of the couch on which the corpse lies and looks down on it*)—may his soul rot in hell.

Adcock stares at him and Pratt meets the stare, challengingly

It's only fair you should know. It'll be in all the papers to-morrow, probably on television to-night. You'll have the press round here in force.

Adcock Oh, Lord. It won't be till to-morrow, I hope.

Pratt Why? What's the difference?

Adcock I can't stand reporters at the best of times. They're all ghouls, even the local ones. And, besides, to-night I'm supposed to be off on a week's holiday. That's why I have to get these files up to date. I've got a locum coming in.

Pratt Where are you going?

Adcock Margate. I've a little dinghy down there.

Pratt Go to-night then. But let us know your movements. We'll want you back for the inquest.

Adcock Of course.

Pratt You're lucky. I won't be able to avoid them. Though this time, I must say, I won't mind so much. You know why?

Adcock (*uncertainly*) I'm sure it's—very important for you . . .

Pratt circles the body again, very slowly

Pratt Yes, it is. They won't be laughing this time. Oh, I feel quite sorry for the press. They'll miss him.

Adcock watches as Pratt talks more to the corpse, or to himself, than to him

He was a very humorous chap, was Jack. The press loved him. He was always good for a story. Used to like writing himself, too. Letters to the papers. With humorous pseudonyms. Like Skypilot, just after the London Airport robbery. Or the Mole, after the Willesden bank job—Do you remember that?

Adcock Yes. I do.

Pratt You would, naturally. It was front page stuff. I went right into the bloody bank while he was there. A tip-off. Everything seemed O.K., I thought they'd been having me on. So I left. And he was in the safe, he'd burrowed through from next door. He was right inside while I was checking the safe door hadn't been tampered with. The public had a right laugh over that. Remember?

Adcock is embarrassed. He does not know what to say

Adcock I—suppose it could have happened to anyone.

Pratt Perhaps. But it happened to me. With Jack, it always happened to me. I was his pet hate, his favourite buffoon. Old Pratt, he always called me.

Pratt pauses, stares at Adcock, who feels he has to say something

Adcock But you did catch him.

Pratt (*sharply*) I don't need to be reminded of that, either. Though for what it's worth, it's the only time he ever was caught. The only time we ever came face to face. For about two minutes. I never even got him to the station and to this day I can't tell you how he slipped those handcuffs, but he did. I knew what the pen-name would be on that occasion before he wrote his bloody letters—Houdini.

Adcock (*delicately*) You—did catch the others.

Pratt (*dismissing it*) Oh, yes. No headlines for them though. They didn't have Jack's glamour. The press likes a bit of glamour. They were just accomplices. Petty crooks. He never told them much. In fact, I'm not sure he didn't shop them himself. Jack liked to work on his own. There must have been two or three he trusted—Christine for one—but not many. No, I didn't get any medals from the press for catching the others but it looked good on the record—they chalked up a lot of bird between them. That didn't worry Jack. And I wasn't going to be satisfied either. There was only one man I wanted.

Pratt stares with smouldering resentment at the corpse. Again Adcock feels he has to say something

Adcock (*politely*) You—put off your retirement, didn't you?
Pratt What?
Adcock Your retirement?
Pratt That's right. For three years, I've been waiting. Oh I earned my keep. I pulled in Klemson and one or two others. They didn't find me funny.

Adcock forces a smile

Adcock Well—you can retire now.
Pratt Yes. Well, almost. There'll be a few things to clear up. There's still half a million in cash from that last bank job. I'd like to find that before I go. But I suppose it's all over really. (*Pause*) Even in death, the bastard cheated me.
Adcock What?
Pratt (*after a pause*) I was close. Getting closer all the time. There was a big reward. We had plenty of informers. And he knew it. I could sense it. I always had a kind of feeling for Jack, for what he was thinking. He was like an eel, a bloody eel. But he knew the trap was closing in . . .

Pratt looks at the body. Adcock waits. Pratt jerks himself out of his thoughts

This afternoon we had a tip. That he was in a hired car, going to London, along this road. I wasn't more than two miles away. We had a road block. All very discreet, of course. Just a census check. (*He walks around the body, then continues*) That's how your police got here so quickly. That's why they called me. Funny, I'd envisaged just about every possibility, except that. It came as a shock. I couldn't believe it at first. D'you know, as we drove here, I was praying that he'd be alive still.
Adcock Mister Pratt, the man is dead!
Pratt He deserved to die! Oh, he'll be buried a bloody hero. The public loved him, cockney boy, sense of humour, made his pile, only took it from the banks, made the coppers look stupid. Banks, police, they're all authority, aren't they? Anyone against them is the underdog. (*Fiercely*) He was a bloody murderer!
Adcock (*shaken*) Murderer?
Pratt Oh, I can't prove it. He was too clever for that. But a lot of people he was connected with just disappeared. He'd use them, and then get rid of them. It's not so difficult. I tell you, there's twice as many murders every year as there are bodies found. Every new motorway has its quota.
Adcock What?
Pratt All those bumps in the road—oh, never mind, Doctor.

The woman's voice is suddenly raised. It is passionate but muffled: we can hardly hear what she says

Christine What the hell is he doing in there? I want to know. I've got a right to know.
Sergeant It's just routine, Miss.

Adcock frowns, remembering his patient

Adcock (*strongly*) Superintendent, I really cannot accept any further delay.

Pratt knows what he is going to say, waves him to stop

Pratt Yes, all right. I'm going. I just wanted to explain to you.

Adcock is a bit lost

Adcock Well—I'm grateful. But my concern now must be for this woman. She's in a hysterical state.

Pratt I had to check, you see? It could all have been an elaborate hoax. Just a trick to get me out of the way. It might not have been Jack at all. I had to make sure.

Adcock Well, now you know.

Pratt Yes, but I want official identification.

Adcock But you've seen him yourself.

Pratt stabs a finger at the body. Adcock is perplexed

Pratt Oh that's him all right, even though he's bloody unrecognizable. But I know Jack. He had a few special characteristics. (*He moves to the body, points to the hand*) Like these three rings. Always wore them. If we'd put it in the papers, he'd have got rid of them. (*He walks away again*) And in any case, I always had a special sort of—feeling—for Jack. I swear if I'd walked into this room, knowing nothing, I'd have known it was him. But that's not good enough. I want an official identification from his wife.

Adcock Why, for God's sake?

Pratt Because then I can retire.

Adcock Well I forbid it.

Pratt You can't.

Adcock Then later . . .

Pratt No. Now.

Pratt opens the door. Adcock looks after him, shocked

Adcock Superintendent, I warn you. If you go through with this, I shall complain that it was specifically against my advice . . .

Pratt Very well, sir . . .

Pratt goes out through the door and Adcock, looking deeply anxious, bites his lip, looking from the door to the body. We see Pratt's figure loom on the frosted glass. His entry provokes movement from the others

Christine (*off*) You again? Haven't you had enough? What did you do? Spit on him?

Pratt (*off*) Come on. In here.

Jennings (*off*) Excuse me, can I go now?

Pratt (*off*) Soon.

There is a final offstage burst of invective from Christine and then Pratt returns, followed by Christine. Christine is attractive, in her late twenties or early thirties. She is lightly bandaged, dishevelled sufficiently to remind us that she has just been in a car crash. She enters boldly, almost aggressively, but then—attention immediately riveted on the body of her husband —determination fails and she sways, puts out a hand to the wall for support. Pratt looks at Christine. His voice is level, expressionless

Sorry to distress you at this time, Mrs Robin, but we would be grateful if you could give evidence of identification.

Christine drags her glance from the body to Pratt. She looks at him with loathing. Pratt moves upstage to the body, stands next to it, one hand gripping the corner of the sheet

Christine Get stuffed.

Christine half gasps, half retches, dragging her hands up to her face to cover her eyes, as Pratt lifts the corner of the sheet. The bulk of Pratt's body prevents the audience from getting a clear view, but we see the bloodstains on the sheet, a sufficiently grim reminder

You know it's Jack, you know it's him . . .

Adcock steps forward, appalled, reproving Pratt fiercely as he moves to put an arm round Christine, who shudders against him

Adcock That was not necessary.

Pratt drops the corner of the sheet. His voice is quite flat

Pratt You must let me be the best judge of that, sir.

Christine pushes Adcock away to stand alone

Christine (*with growing anger*) He's just a bloody sadist, didn't you know?

Adcock looks anxious. Pratt is unmoved

Jack always said so. That's why he used to take it out on you. And now this is all you can do, isn't it, to get back at him?

Adcock tries to take her arm, calm her. Christine brushes him away impatiently. Her fury is directed only against Pratt. She takes a step towards him

Go on then, gorge yourself. Do you think I'm afraid to look at him just because he's dead, mashed up? If he were a stinking corpse, he'd smell sweeter than you ever could, or any other bloody copper. (*She screams at him*) Bastard!

Christine moves forward to attack Pratt who, quickly, easily grasps her upraised wrists. Adcock hurries to part them and Pratt surrenders her to the doctor

Pratt Give her a shot. She's hysterical.

Adcock starts to lead Christine away. He is still angry

Adcock What the hell do you expect?

Christine halts him. Her fury has gone now. She is quiet, pleading

Christine No—please . . .

She indicates that she wants to go back to the body. Adcock is reluctant but lets her go, moving with her, glancing warningly at Pratt, who keeps well away—but watching closely all the time

(*murmuring*) Jack—Jack . . . (*She sobs quietly. Her shoulders rise and fall as she represses over-emotion*)

Adcock glares at Pratt as he escorts the bowed, sobbing Christine towards the door. Pratt shrugs minutely

Adcock and Christine go out

Pratt drops the sheet and starts towards the door

Pratt Sergeant! My car!

Adcock enters

Adcock You could have waited. At least until they'd time to wash the body.

Pratt does not answer

Can I make arrangements now? For the body to be removed?
Pratt Yes. Sorry to have inconvenienced you, Doctor.
Adcock What about Mrs Robin?
Pratt She'll get over it. Jack left her well provided for, I bet.
Adcock That is not what I meant.
Pratt Oh—I'll see she gets to hospital.

Pratt goes out, leaving Adcock in silent fury

(*off*) Right, come on . . .
Christine (*off*) Where now? The nick?
Pratt (*off*) Just the hospital. For a check-up. Sergeant see to her.
Sergeant Yes, sir. Come along, Miss.

Pratt enters

Pratt Have a good holiday!

Pratt exits, ~~followed by Adcock~~ Adcock goes to desk

There are the sounds of muffled voices again, doors slamming, engines starting up, cars driving away

Adcock's silhouette is seen, alone, in the back room. Then the light in the back room goes out

After a pause, Adcock comes back into the surgery. He moves to the desk, hesitates, then picks up the telephone. He has his back to the corpse

ow I st phone the (margin handwriting)

Adcock Coroner's office? Mr Powell, please . . .

The corpse suddenly rises, and the sheet falls away from his face, a ghastly bloody mess. The head turns towards Adcock, as—

the CURTAIN *falls*

SCENE 2

The same. As the CURTAIN *rises we see Adcock slumped in his chair, head in arms on the desk. The bloodstained sheet lies casually across the foot of the orthopaedic table*

Jack enters. He carries a week-end case, bloodstained shirt and dinner jacket, and has a towel around his neck

Adcock starts and sits bolt upright. He stares, nervously at Jack, whose face still bears terrible scars. In height and build, Jack is about the same size as the doctor, with a cheerful open countenance, an infectious grin. His easy manner contrasts strongly with the doctor's nervous intensity

Jack All right, then?
Adcock Yes.
Jack Thought you was having a kip? (*He hangs the jacket and shirts on the hooks*)
Adcock No. I'm just—totally exhausted.
Jack 'Ere, open this up for us. My hands are all frozen. What stuff did you use?
Adcock (*opening the suitcase*) Ethyl chloride.
Jack I've had a right job too, getting this muck off.
Adcock You need a special cream.
Jack Mickey'll fix me up when he gets back.
Adcock Is that wise?
Jack What?
Adcock For him to come back here?
Jack That's all right. We know what we're doing.
Adcock I hope you do.
Jack Getting worried?
Adcock (*angrily*) What the hell do you think?
Jack I think you're getting worried.
Adcock They'll be here at half-past eight.

Jack unpacks the suitcase and sets up a small shaving mirror. As the dialogue proceeds, he peels off the plastic scars and cleans off the make-up

Jack We'll be ready. Don't worry. It's all over now bar the shouting. And you did your bit a treat.

Adcock (*with a grunt*) Hm—At least three times I thought I was going to have a heart attack.

Jack Did you? I don't think I ever got worried once. Not even while old Pratt was looking down at me. Mind you I nearly burst out laughing. Good thing I had that rib cage on under my shirt, he would have seen me breathing for certain—and all those aliases! But he left out my real name. Johny Rawlings. Mind you, I prefer Jack Robin. It's like a film star, you know. That's the name that made me famous.

Adcock (*after a pause*) Do you mean it?

Jack What?

Adcock That you nearly burst out laughing?

Jack Yes. Of course. I tell you, if there hadn't been so much riding on it, I'd have been seriously tempted to have a giggle. Can't you imagine? While he was checking on my rings? If I'd suddenly sat up and said: watch it, Pratty, that's twenty four carat. No nicking, now.

Adcock, in spite of his nervousness, is obliged to smile at the thought. Jack chuckles with him

Or with the sheet, you know. Pratt, I have come to haunt you. For persecuting me in my life time. Poor old sod would have had a heart attack—come to think of it, that might have been the best way round. Killed him off instead of me.

Adcock Why? Would that have made any difference? He didn't really persecute you, did he?

Jack I don't know. I suppose you could say I persecuted him.

Adcock That's what he thinks.

Jack I know. I heard him. Really took it to heart, didn't he?

Adcock You made a fool of him.

Jack It was only for a giggle. If I'd taken him seriously, I'd have been a bloody nervous wreck. All that bull about not retiring, spending the rest of his life hunting me down and so on.

Adcock He's a very determined man.

Jack Bit neurotic, if you ask me. Still, you're the doctor. You tell me. You must admit he seemed a bit relieved, all this being over.

Adcock But it's not over.

Jack You know it. I know it. But Pratt doesn't. That's the important thing.

Adcock He's just one man.

Jack He's the man in charge of the investigation. What he says, goes. You're just feeling guilty, love. That's why you're nervous.

Adcock Christ, I'm feeling that all right.

Jack I don't know why. You did a great job. Beautiful. I'd never have thought it of you. A natural. Really—I'll tell you something now it's all over . . .

Adcock It's not all over. I keep telling you.

Jack (*with equanimity*) All right, now it's nearly all over, I'll tell you. We were really worried about you. Straight. I didn't like the idea of using you at all.

Adcock (*bitterly*) Then why did you?

Jack Had to, didn't we? We needed a doctor, someone in just the right position. We were lucky finding you. I can't tell you: dead lucky.

Adcock How the hell did you find me?

Jack That'd be telling. But we've got a list—a kind of register, you know—all sorts of people. Dodgy doctors, crooked solicitors. Professional people, fronters, you know what I mean?

Adcock I do now, God help me.

Jack Don't be like that. I'm doing you a favour if you think about it.

Adcock Is that another of your jokes?

Jack stops what he is doing, turns to look at the doctor. A compelling change takes place when he is not employing his usual light banter. Jack serious, looks a different person, one very much to be reckoned with, mean, bordering on vicious. His gaze is level, penetrating. The voice has authority

Jack No, Doctor Adcock, it's not. I don't always kid, just most of the time. Because that's me. That's the way I like it to be. Only sometimes people take liberties, they don't think you can be serious about anything. Do you know what I mean?

Adcock (*nervously*) I didn't mean any offence . . .

Jack (*hard on him*) No—you didn't mean any offence. You were just talking down to me. And I don't think you've got any cause to talk down to me.

Adcock No. I wasn't.

Jack Shut up, mate, and listen. You don't get on that list by accident, you know. You're not a name picked out of a hat or a number taken out of the phone book. You get there for a reason.

Adcock Yes. I understand.

Jack Well I don't think you do or you wouldn't try and be funny with me when I tell you I'm doing you a favour. You might be a respectable man in this village, cock, but all I know is that you're a back room abortionist and a bloody dope pusher.

Adcock That's not true!

Jack No? It might not be now, but it was. And now you're paying for it, mate.

Adcock You wouldn't understand, I tried to help people, that's all.

Jack (*viciously*) Come off it! What, help poor girls, at a hundred and fifty quid a time?

Adcock I didn't only do it for the money.

Jack None do, mate. But the money helps, doesn't it? Especially when it's tax free. If you wanted to help, why didn't you operate at the local clinic? It's all legal these days, isn't it?

Adcock For God's sake, not everyone wants to go to . . .

Jack I know. I know all about it, mate. I had a young sister like that. She was terrified my old man would find out about it and give her a good hiding, and the boyfriend—and he would! So she nicked the money from me and went to someone like you. Oh, it was all very quiet, very discreet. None of us knew a bloody thing until I heard her moaning, found her lying in a pool of blood in her bedroom, two o'clock in the morning—he'd botched it up. They told her at the hospital. She'd paid a hundred and fifty quid of my money and the hospital had to finish off the job properly.

Adcock (*shaken*) Was she—all right?

Jack Oh, she got over it all right. Silly cow got herself pregnant again six months afterwards. Same twit. Only this time she married him. Poor bastard. He knew he'd be in for a right pasting if he didn't. So they've lived unhappily ever after. But that's not the point, mate. She was my sister. And she nearly died, I'm telling you, it was touch and go. And all because of someone like you.

Adcock Well there is no point in trying to explain to you. As I said before I wouldn't expect you to understand.

Jack rises to face him, belligerently

Jack Oh? Why not? Am I so pig ignorant? If you ask me, cock, you're the one who doesn't understand. You don't know what people like us think of people like you. You think you're so bloody respectable. Public school, I suppose? And a doctor—do you want to know what you are to me? I'll tell you. Shit!

Adcock sees no point in arguing. He shrugs and turns away, but this only serves to infuriate Jack

Yes, I mean, I'm a crook, right? Anti-social. I steal money. And I don't care who I steal it from so long as it's someone who's got it. But I do mean, who's got it. Banks, insurance companies, big factories. They're all stinking rich and I just spread it around a bit. People like them have been robbing people like me all our lives and they'll go on doing it: only I hit back, that's all.

Adcock is scared of Jack but he tries to hide it, assert an intellectual superiority at least

Adcock If you see yourself as some kind of Robin Hood . . .

Jack That's where you're wrong. I don't, and never have done. If you're talking about someone who robbed from the rich to give to the poor, which I doubt he ever did anyway. Errol Flynn might have done but not this Robin, mate. I steal from the rich to give to me and mine and sod the poor. If they had any sense they'd do the same. But they're not going to ponce on me. But I never knocked any old ladies on the head, to break into their gas meters, or stole handbags in the street. And I never extorted money from pregnant girls or pushed bloody pills, because that's what I call dirty.

Adcock It's easy to talk like that if you don't know the facts.

Jack I know. Oh, I know, cock. Do you think I've never seen them, queuing up for their prescriptions Thursday at midnight like a lot of bloody refugees. Running to the nearest phone-box or toilet to give themselves a fix while they're still sane enough to do it?

Adcock Then you should understand . . .

Jack I understand that people like you give them their prescriptions. Why don't you let them stand on their own two feet, even if it is till they drop and die? Because that's what they're going to do, anyway. What do you call them, social inadequates? Weren't they equally bloody socially inadequate before people like you handed out so-called life-savers at two a penny? How'd they manage then? What was the worst they could do? Commit suicide? Well why not let the poor sods do it and get it over with?

Adcock Because they can be helped. They can be pulled through. They are not social inadequates—and we don't practice euthanasia in this country.

Jack (*after a pause*) You think I don't know what that means, don't you?

Adcock I'm sure you do.

Jack I do and I'm not talking about euthanasia, I'm talking about people being able to do themselves in if they want to—which is perfectly legal.

Adcock Everyone has a different point of view.

Jack Right. And I'll tell you mine. Because I get 'em, these kids you're so-called trying to help. Because I've got money, and that's what they want, to pay people like you.

Adcock I never sold drugs.

Jack You fed them, mate. And you earned a living out of it. Give yourself any motive you like: you don't have to answer to me. But don't try and kid me either. Because I've had young girls offering their stinking scarred bodies to me for anything I wanted, so long as I'd stake them. And boys who'd commit bloody murder for me just to get the bread for another fix. And I mean that, murder! So you've got nothing to be proud about, doctor.

Adcock I didn't say I was proud.

Jack Right. And if you didn't know you hadn't done wrong, you wouldn't have hidden yourself in this God-forsaken place. The boys got on to you, didn't they? Put the screws on a bit?

Adcock They tried to blackmail me.

Jack Tried? They succeeded. They made you run, anyway. And don't think you got away, mate. You didn't. They knew where you were, and they'd have been down to see you. Only I found out. And I bought them off. Because I needed you.

Adcock (*defensively*) Well, I did what you wanted.

Jack, quite abruptly, is good humoured again

Jack That's right. That's what I'm telling you. It all worked a treat. You're a born actor. I believed every word you said. And so did old Pratty, which is more to the point.

Adcock I still think you're mad. You'll never pull this off. (*He takes a pill-box from the trolley*)

Jack Why not? You put in the bit about going off on holiday. So no-one's

going to miss you. And you've got this little boat which you bought
out of earnings which we won't enquire about. Perfect. The little boat
overturns and everybody says poor old Doctor Adcock, what a lovely
feller he was.

Adcock And the inquest?

Jack (*politely*) On me, or you?

Adcock On you.

Jack So you're not around to give evidence. It's what they call a double
tragedy. I mean, you've already done your job, haven't you? Certified
I was dead.

Adcock It's not as simple as that.

Jack I don't see why not. A few awkward technicalities as you might say,
but they can't leave me hanging about on ice, can they? I mean to say,
I've got to have a decent burial sometime or Christine'll do her nut.
(*He chuckles*) Wasn't she the greatest? I tell you, she brought tears to
my eyes. She did, straight. I hope she's not going to carry on like that
when I do go. I'll feel guilty in my grave.

Adcock (*stiffly*) Yes. She was very convincing.

Jack I'm not kidding, love, if I didn't have other plans I'd give up my
game, put you both on the stage up West.

Adcock goes to the desk with the pills and picks up a glass of milk

Adcock I'm afraid I've got other plans, too.

Jack Yes. Shame, that.

Adcock drinks

'Ere, you want to keep off that sherbert. It won't do you any good. Still,
think how well off you'll be. Forty grand, you can start up anywhere
you like. One of the South Sea Islands. No better not. There might not
be much demand for your trade there. Try one of the Catholic countries.

Adcock If you want to know, I'm thinking of going to Africa.

Jack Very good. Mission work. The old Doctor Schweizer bit, eh?
How's your organ playing?

Adcock Pratt was right about you. (*He takes a holdall from the floor and
puts it on the couch*)

Jack Was he? Right about what?

Jack goes back to continue removing the grease paint from his face

Adcock (*taking a sweater and gymshoes from the holdall*) You've got a distorted sense of humour. (*He puts the pill-box in the holdall*)

Jack Depends what you think is right in the first place, doesn't it? I saw
this play on the telly a couple of weeks ago, where this girl's having an
op. on her face and she's terrified she's going to come out of it dead
ugly. She's all bandaged up, like. The doctors and nurses have all got
masks on. Then she comes round and they take off the bandages. And
she's beautiful, really beautiful. She asks for a mirror, first thing,
naturally and when she looks in it, she screams her head off. Because it's
all on another planet, see, where people have got no noses and funny

twisted mouths and that's normal. So what she sees is abnormal. Which is why she screams. (*Pause*) Did you see it?

Adcock No.

Jack But you get the point?

Adcock Yes. (*He changes his shoes*)

Jack So you can't talk about distorted. It depends where you're looking from. I like a bit of a laugh but some people don't always think it funny. Especially Pratt.

Adcock He's no fool, you know.

Jack Who, Pratt? (*He studies himself in the mirror*) Here, do you think I've got all this off?

Adcock, unwillingly, looks up to inspect him

Adcock Yes.

Jack Wasn't that a fantastic make-up job? I tell you, when I first looked in the mirror, it scared the hell out of me.

Adcock Yes.

Jack Funny things, that's what made me think of that T.V. play. I sort of realized how that girl felt.

Adcock Yes.

Jack You're a great conversationalist, aren't you?

Adcock I didn't think I was being employed to chat.

Jack Well only to Pratty, and you've done that.

Adcock All right then, all I want to do now is to get away from here. (*He puts his shoes in the holdall and replaces it on the floor*)

Jack I'm not stopping you, mate. But they've got to come and collect the body yet. And anyway, you've got to stick to the timetable, leave to-night. You've made all your arrangements, haven't you?

Adcock Yes. What about the body?

Jack What about it?

Adcock (*with a sudden burst of fury*) For God's sake, stop treating me like an idiot. You blackmailed me into doing this and I had no choice but I still don't see how you think you're going to get away with it.

Jack That's because you're you. It's what we were talking about. You've got a certain point of view, you see, and you only look at things one way.

Adcock Well what other way is there?

Jack There's my way.

Adcock (*despairingly*) Your way!

Jack (*hard again*) Yes, my way, and that's the way that counts. Because it's my knowledge, my experience, that's going to let us all get away with this. So don't worry about it, doctor. Stand on me.

Adcock God help us.

Jack That's up to him, isn't it? I'm not a religious man myself but if he wants to weigh in, I don't mind. But I'm not asking him. You please yourself. I put my faith in Jack Robin, if you don't mind.

Adcock (*with a sigh*) Well—I've got to hand it to you . . .

Jack That's more like it, doctor. Have a little bit of admiration. That's where the old Pratt always went wrong. He had to try and be more clever than me always. And he's not. So his point of view was all wrong, do you see?

Adcock I'm beginning to.

Jack Clever feller. You're catching on.

Adcock Fast. (*He puts on the sweater*)

Jack (*drily*) Well, don't get carried away. But you're catching on. (*He turns to lecture Adcock*) You see, I'll explain. There's two types of crime you can get away with. One is what the newspapers always call meticulously planned. That's my trademark almost. And it's a lot of graft, I tell you, a lot of organization. I sometimes think I waste my time, the work I put into these jobs. I could be organizing a big factory or something, getting twenty grand a year honest. Only it wouldn't pay me. It's the tax, isn't it? Robs you of all incentive. Well you ought to know. (*Having thoroughly cleaned himself up, he puts the various cleaning items back in the case*)

Adcock Don't start on that again.

Jack (*putting the dirty sheet in the case and taking out the clean one*) All right, if you're touchy.Then the other way is what the same newspapers call breath-taking audacity. And that's another trade-mark of mine. Probably the one that worries Pratt most, because it makes him look a burke—I'm telling you, it's marvellous what you can get away with if you've got the nerve . : . Are you listening?

Adcock I haven't got much choice.

Jack (*putting the clean sheet on the couch*) Right. But don't get stroppy about it or I might get the needle to you again—I was telling you. This mate of mine, he was getting married, see? And his bird wanted this big couch, all in black leather. It put him in a bit of a cleft stick because he wanted to see her right, naturally, but at the same time, he was skint. And he didn't want to go and break the Times Furnishing window on his stag night, in case we all got nicked and he missed his bit of the other on his wedding night. Naturally. Right?

Adcock Yes.

Jack This was a long time ago. I mean now, I'd let him pick what he wanted out of Harrods. But I was on the ribs, too. So you know what we done?

Adcock No.

Jack We all put on white overalls, steamed up to London Airport, marched in and picked up a couple of sofas out of the main lounge. And no-one even stopped us. We put them on the van we'd nicked and drove off. Simple. But someone had to think it out.

Adcock You, no doubt.

Jack No. It wasn't. But it taught me a lesson I'll never forget. And that's what we've worked this time. A bit of both. A lot of planning over a long time. And then the breathless audacious bit. (*He changes the pillow-case for the clean one from the case*)

Adcock I still don't see . . .

Jack How we're going to get away with it. I know. And I keep telling you we already have. So long as we don't overlook a single detail.

Adcock Like?

Jack Like for example, it occurs to me that when my nut hit that windscreen, some of this make-up must have come off. So tonight Mick'll have to break into the garage and make sure. Do you see?

Adcock Yes. I'm impressed.

Jack And so you should be. Learn what it's like to be on the other side, doctor. We have to work too. I mean, imagine. How long this took to work out.

Adcock It's ingenious, so far as it goes.

Jack It's ingenious all the way. I had to find Micky, for a start. A marvellous stunt man. The greatest. And he had to find the make-up contact. And that contact couldn't know what it was all about. (*He takes the cotton-wool and surgical spirit from the case*)

Adcock Difficult.

Jack (*cleaning the side of the couch with spirit*) No more than finding you. In fact, the same job. You and Micky. Both crooked, but without records. That wasn't easy.

Adcock No. (*He hangs his coat on a hook and transfers his wallet from it to his anorak*)

Jack No. And then we had to get old Pratt all steamed up, thinking he was hot on our trail, which I must admit he was, the old git, so that wasn't difficult.

Adcock He's not a stupid man.

Jack So you keep saying, and I don't know why you think I think he is stupid, because I don't. He's clever, crafty and cunning. But he'll never beat me. He never could. He forced a draw, as you might say, once or twice, but that was his lot. (*He puts back the spirit*)

Adcock You think he'll hold those two?

Jack (*taking the dustpan and brush from the case*) No. He can't hold Micky for anything, because he's clean. I've had Micky in training for this job for a year now. All that bit, about him working for a car-hire firm. It's all dead straight, right on the line. Now, Christine, he will be naughty with, or he'll try to be. But you heard him yourself, he'll never be able to hold her for long. She's the innocent victim, the loving wife. He knows. (*He sweeps the floor by the couch*)

Adcock Clever.

Jack Bloody clever, mate. And I needed to be, to put it over old Pratt, because believe me, I know he's no mug.

Adcock Then what makes you think that when I disappear . . .?

Jack That he won't suspect? Of course he will. But by then, I'll have him. He'll have opened his trap to the press, about how he got me in the end, the end being the operative word like. The silly old sod will have started on his retirement at last in a blaze of glory. Now what d'you think he's going to do? Come back and spend the rest of his life looking for me? Open up the case again? Believe me, he'll let sleeping dogs lie. I might stop all his sweet dreams in his retirement, but that'll be all.

Adcock I see you're a psychologist too.

Jack I don't pretend to be anything I'm not. And I'm not an educated person. I don't particularly want to be. But if you mean I know how

people react, yes I do. I have to. And I know I've spiked Pratt. Right up
his jacksy. (*He puts the dustpan in the case and takes out the plastic bag*)
Adcock You're taking a big risk.
Jack That's a stupid bloody thing to say, love. My whole life's been a
risk. That's what crime is, it's like motor racing. One bad crash and you're
finished. And he'd have caught up with me all right, the Pratt. Only this
time his informants were planted by me. I wanted him to get close.
Because I was setting him up. But it was dodgy. I put my life in Mick's
hands, mate, and Christine's too. (*Jack gives Adcock the plastic bag to
hold, into which he wants to empty the dustpan*) Hold this will you. That
crash wasn't faked, it was real. But it was controlled you see. That's
the difference. That's the risk. (*Jack takes the plastic bag from Adcock,
thanks him*) And I'll tell you the biggest risk of all. You. (*He deposits the
plastic bag in the suitcase and grins*) But you came through with flying
colours, Doctor Adcock, and I'd like to shake your hand.

*Jack walks towards the desk, suddenly stops, winces, hobbles a foot or two,
then stops, rests one hand on the edge of the desk, reaches down to slip off
his shoe*

Blimey.
Adcock What's the matter?
Jack I don't know. But it bloody hurts. (*He feels inside the shoe*) Thought
so. A nail. Funny, isn't it?
Adcock Funny?
Jack The details. The little things. You plan everything. But some things
just happen. I mean, suppose I suddenly had to make a run for it. I
mean literally, physically run. I'd be nearly crippled. Just because of a
little nail. Got a hammer?
Adcock What?
Jack A hammer?
Adcock Look, I've made arrangements with the coroner's office . . .
Jack Good.
Adcock Their men will be here at half-past eight.
Jack Well you'll want me out of it then, won't you? And I'm not going
to play bloody Hopalong Cassidy. I mean I've already had a nasty car
crash and died. That's enough discomfort for one day, isn't it?
Adcock (*distractedly*) I've got one somewhere.
Jack (*cheerfully*) Good.

Adcock starts to leave the room

Don't worry so much.

Adcock stares at him

It's all going like a dream.

Adcock shakes his head, and leaves the room

(*calling after him*) It's just the clock ticking away that bugs you. Forget
it. Some people are time conscious, some aren't. Some run down the

platform at one-thirty to catch the one-forty. Others stroll through the barrier at one-thirty-nine. Different philosophies. You know what I mean?

There is no answer. Just the sound of drawers being opened in an adjoining room. Jack studies himself in the mirror for a moment, with a certain amount of vanity. Then, humming quietly to himself, he slips off the rings from his fingers, one at a time, places them neatly on the desk

Adcock returns, carrying a claw hammer

Adcock I'm sorry. Is this too big?
Jack No, it's lovely. Thanks.

Jack occupies himself, with some concentration, to working the hammer into the shoe. He cannot beat the hammer inside so he has to place it so that he can hammer the sole with his fist against the hammerhead used as an anvil. It is an involved piece of business. Adcock paces the floor nervously. The whole business of the shoe irritates him immensely. Once or twice, he stops as though to say something, but thinks better of it. Jack reacts to him however

What's on your mind?
Adcock Nothing.
Jack (*casually*) You're all set, aren't you?
Adcock Yes. Well . . .
Jack I mean—you did just like I told you, right? Everyone knows you're going down on your boat. You take off quietly on the night tide. Right?
Adcock Yes.
Jack Great.
Adcock Except . . .
Jack What?
Adcock Well, the body.
Jack What about it?
Adcock They'll be here, to collect it.
Jack I know. It's all arranged. I told you.
Adcock (*with a nervous explosion*) Well where the hell is it?
Jack It'll be here. Any time now. I promise you.
Adcock You murdered someone, didn't you?
Jack What?
Adcock You murdered someone?
Jack You don't have to go into that. That's another department.
Adcock He said you were a murderer.

Jack grins, examines the shoe, tries it out, nods delight

Jack Beautiful. What did you say?
Adcock Nothing.
Jack Yes, you did. I heard you the first time. Now you've done a good job so far, doctor. Don't start giving me problems.
Adcock All right. I don't want to. Just give me my money and let me go.
Jack You've still got a bit to do, haven't you? And then you'll get paid.

When it's all over. My boys are down at Margate. When you arrive, they'll pay you. You don't think I'm going to cheat you, do you?

Adcock No. No.

Jack You say that like you mean yes. (*Jack tosses the hammer to Adcock*) Here, catch. You disappoint me, doctor. I mean suddenly, you've sort of broken up.

Adcock How the hell can you be so calm? (*He puts the hammer on the couch*)

Jack Ah, well, that's a matter of what they call personal philosophy.

Adcock Rubbish!

Jack What's the matter? What's bugging you? You won't get caught. I guarantee it.

Adcock How can you guarantee it?

Jack Because I know what I'm doing.

Adcock You know! You know everything. You think you're some kind of tin god, pulling strings to make people move exactly the way you want them to move. (*His jagged nerves finally give way. He yells*) You want to know why I'm a nervous wreck. I'll tell you. Because you're a bloody paranoiac!

Jack (*startled*) Eh?

Adcock You think you can get away with murder, but you can't!

Jack (*calmly*) I'm only killing myself.

Adcock It was all worked out. The perfect make-up job. The perfect car smash. The perfect statement of death from the perfect doctor. The perfect death scene acted out by the perfect wife. And then the perfect alibi, the perfect body to be buried. No doubt someone your height, your build. Identified by your wife in the presence of a police superintendent. Both perfect witnesses.

Jack (*mildly*) Are you trying to say I've committed the perfect crime? I'd say you were perfectly right.

Adcock (*viciously*) Well I'd say you were wrong. I was going to keep my mouth shut, take my money, go away, but I can't take any more of your bloody arrogance. Let me tell you something for a change. There's one part of your calculations that's not perfect.

Jack You're beginning to worry me, doctor. What's that?

Adcock That body is going to be re-examined, and Coroners aren't quite the simpletons you seem to take them to be. That corpse you have has probably been dead a day or more. And a doctor can judge death within a couple of hours.

Jack Well I know that. When I go into something, I go into it thoroughly.

Adcock (*appalled*) My God, you don't mean you had someone all set up . . .?

Jack I had to, didn't I?

Adcock Christ, Pratt was right about you.

Jack That wasn't very nice, doctor, the bit about me being paranoiac. Just because I'm efficient and work things out.

Adcock I can't go through with this. I can't.

Jack You'll be all right. You'll be fine. Look on the desk.

Adcock, appalled but fascinated, looks and sees the rings

Adcock Your rings.

Jack That's right. I mean, I was going to spare you the details. But you've hurt me now. I mean, suggesting I'd slipped up. I never slip up. Or if I do, I always pick myself up. Now about the facial injuries . . .

Adcock (*turning his face away*) I don't want to know.

Jack I thought you were a bit squeamish. That's why I made out I had the nail in my shoe. (*He picks up the hammer*) This is what I'm going to use, see? For the corpse. Mash up the face a bit.

Adcock cannot prevent himself from looking at the hammer

Sit at Desk

Adcock (*revolted*) God.

Jack It's all been worked out. I'll explain to you if you like . . .

Adcock No! (*Hoarsely, pleading*) No. Please. Just let me go now.

Jack looks at Adcock, shakes his head chidingly

Jack I guessed you'd break down. That's why I didn't want to use you. But I had to. You had the perfect background. Local doctor. Just arrived, Not too well known. The perfect set-up.

Adcock clutches his head, nearly hysterical

Adcock All right, all right. Why can't we get on with it.

Jack (*chiding*) You didn't let me finish, doctor. You also had the perfect height and the perfect build.

Adcock's hands claw down his face, hysteria frozen by a new all consuming fear as he stares unbelievingly at Jack

(*quietly*) Yes. *You.*

Jack advances on Adcock, the claw hammer upraised, as—

the CURTAIN *falls*

ACT II

Scene 1

The living-room of a small modern flat, devoid of furniture. Afternoon

A door in the back wall leads to a small hall and the front door. Next to that door there is a fitted cupboard. Another door leads to the bedroom and kitchen. By the window is a pair of steps. Draped across it are some curtains, half ready to hang. There is a large carpet which has been dumped, ready to lay

As the Curtain *rises the front door is heard to open and close. A pause, then Christine enters. She carries a fairly bulky paper parcel. She moves straight to the window. Balancing the parcel awkwardly, she cranes to peer out of the window, across the street. Then she turns away from the window, biting her lower lip as though in nervous doubt. There is the sound of a train passing. She becomes aware of the parcel in her arms and looks around for somewhere to put it. She then puts it in the cupboard, goes to the tea-chest, puts her handbag on the floor and takes off her coat*

Jack starts to open the front door, Christine turns and sees it opening. She gasps. Jack enters with a champagne bottle and stands there grinning

Christine Oh, my God . . . (*She puts her coat over the back of the chair by the tea-chest*)

Jack Surprise, surprise.

Jack moves into the room. Christine is still getting back her breath from the shock of finding him there

Christine You must be mad.

Jack Eh?

Christine What are you doing here?

Jack I came to see you, didn't I? It's been a long time. (*He kisses her*) Five weeks.

Christine (*pulling away from him*) But Pratt's outside.

Jack Oh yes?

Christine He's following me.

Jack He don't give up, do he?

Christine Jack, he might come up!

Jack (*calmly*) That's all right. Now stop worrying! Stand on Jack. I have missed you.

Christine is not too anxious to succumb to this embrace. She holds him off

Christine Jack, please, you've got to get out of here. I'm telling you, Pratt's following me everywhere. He even came up here but I wouldn't answer the door.

Jack I know.

Christine What?

Jack Yes. (*Thumbing towards the back wall*) I'm living in the next door flat, see. I've been watching him.

Christine You've been what! Have you gone right out of your mind?

Jack (*putting the bottle on the floor*) Why? What d'you think I had you move in here for? You don't think I'd tell you to buy a crummy gaff like this, do you? Unless there was a reason?

Christine But suppose he comes up again?

Jack Suppose he does? Anyway, I'm dead.

Christine cannot avoid a shudder at the phrase

Christine Oh, Jack, don't!

Jack (*mock seriously*) Well you might as well face up to it, love.

Christine (*really serious*) You don't know how I've faced up to it. I had to go through the whole awful funeral ceremony.

Jack (*interested*) Oh yes, I was going to ask you. Did it go off well?

Christine It was horrible. I don't even want to think about it.

Jack (*coaxing*) Oh go on, tell us. It was my funeral.

Christine It was like a nightmare. But real. (*She reproves him*) How can you just stand there chatting like this?

Jack It's my savoir faire. (*He winks at her*) I should like to have been there. You know, to pay my respects. Did I get plenty of flowers?

Christine Hundreds. From people I never even heard of.

Jack Yes, well I was always very popular.

Christine Like Joan? And Evelyn?

Jack's hesitation is only fractional

Jack Distant cousins. Nice of them to think of me. (*Changing the subject quickly*) I bet my old Auntie Lily was there.

Christine Sobbing her eyes out.

Jack Bloody old hypocrite. She always hated my guts. Who else was there?

Christine Moysher, Freddy, all that lot.

Jack (*touched*) You never know who your friends are, do you, until you're in trouble?

Christine And our friend Pratt. He was there of course.

Jack Well naturally. I was the best P.R. man he ever had. He suffered a great loss, old Pratty.

Christine You can joke. Do you know, he watched that coffin every inch into the grave?

Jack Well he would, wouldn't he? Expecting me to pop up at any moment. The great escape artist. I wouldn't be surprised if he didn't nip back at midnight with one of them ready-mix concrete tip-ups. Good luck and good-bye, Jack, and here's half a ton of cement to make sure.

Christine (*shuddering again*) Oh, stop it. (*She goes to the window, looks out. Whatever she sees, startles her*) Jack!

Jack What?

Christine He's gone

Jack Gone where?

Christine I mean he's not standing there. And he's not in his car either.

Jack Perhaps he's hiding underneath it? Look and see if his big feet are poking out.

Christine (*angrily*) Oh stop joking! Suppose he does come up?

Jack I want him to come up.

Christine *What!?*

A train passes

Jack Why act suspicious, like pretending you're not here? Be truthful. Here's you, poor little Christine, breadwinner gone, fallen on hard times, forced to move into tatty Willesden drum. Puts him off the track, don't it?

Christine Nothing puts him off. Why does he keep on following me? He's supposed to be retired now.

Jack Yes, I heard it on the radio. Laugh, weren't it?

Christine (*distracted, gnawing her lower lip*) I only saw it in the papers.

Jack (*cheerful, quite the opposite from Christine*) Oh, you missed something. He was on himself. Fame at last. How he's seen off Jack and now he was going to live in a cottage in the country, keep bees or something. What's he know about bees?

Christine I don't trust him, Jack.

Jack Quite right. Never trust any copper. They're all villains. But he's not with the fuzz any more now, is he? He's bought it, sold out, retired. Here, what did he say at the inquest?

Christine Oh that was awful.

Jack (*eager*) Yes?

Christine He just sat there, his eyes boring into me. Just as if he was—reading my mind.

Jack Ah, you don't want to take any notice of that. It's a typical rozzer's trick. They couldn't read tea leaves in a cup.

Christine (*remembering*) And he kept on. Even after the funeral. He came to see me.

Jack Yes? What about?

Christine The money. That's what he said, anyway.

Jack Ah, well now that makes him feel really sore. It was only half a victory for him, wasn't it, me going the way I did? And not being able to clear up the business of the money, that reduced it to a quarter. That's probably why he's still keeping on. It's a matter of personal pride, you see? He can't help it. He's got an inferiority complex. And you can understand why.

Christine Why?

Jack Well he is inferior, isn't he? Anyway, never mind about him, love.

Let's talk about ourselves. (*He pulls Christine into an embrace and this time she does not resist*) Oh, I have missed you.

Christine You don't know how I've missed you. If I'd known you were next door, when I came here yesterday—(*she is half laughing, half crying*) —I'd have clawed the walls down.

Jack (*with sincerity*) I couldn't let you know, love. I didn't dare. I had to let the first week pass, suss it all out like. I mean, that's the kind of discipline you've got to have.

Christine When can we go, Jack? When can we leave?

Jack We've got to stick to the timetable. Next week, when you move in here official like, all them geysers in white overalls carrying your gear up and down the stairs, that's when we'll slip away. That's when they'll least expect it.

Christine Till then I've got to go back every evening?

Jack That's right. Just like you have been doing. Watch the telly, have a few callers round, sympathizing. You've got to play it all out, love.

Christine turns her head away

Christine Oh, Jack . . .

The doorbell rings. Christine's body goes rigid

(*Whispering*) Jack!

Jack is calm but the tone of his voice has an equal urgency

Jack Don't flap!
Christine It's Pratt!

Jack moves across to the cupboard. He is still calm, but quick

Jack Good. Look, now let him in. I'll hide in there. Now remember, whatever happens, I don't exist. Like I told you before. Believe in what you say and you'll act it natural. I don't exist. I'm not here. *O.K?*

Christine's head turns to the door as the bell rings again. Jack pulls her back to face him

O.K?

Christine nods dumbly. Jack gives her a reassuring grin, steps into the cupboard with the parcel and shuts the door. Christine goes towards the front door, then sees the champagne bottle. She picks it up and opens the cupboard door

Jack Oh my Gawd! (*He takes the bottle and shuts the door*)

The doorbell rings again

Christine Coming. (*She looks round desperately for some sort of prop then sees an overall draped across the carpet. She quickly slips it on and goes towards the front door, leaving the room door open*)

The front door is heard to open

Pratt (*off*) Can I come in?
Christine No, you can't.
Pratt Thank you.

Pratt bulldozes his way past her into the room. Christine follows him in, tight-lipped. Pratt takes a good look around the room

Christine I suppose it's the only way I'll get rid of you.
Pratt (*cheerfully*) That's right.

Christine enters after Pratt. She moves straight to the pair of steps, starts to thread hooks into the curtains. Pratt stands at the door for a moment, half smiling, taking a good look around

Pratt Surprised to see me?
Christine (*coldly*) You must be joking. Do you think I didn't spot you standing on the pavement opposite all day yesterday? Why the change of tactics?
Pratt (*after a pause*) It got a bit nippy.
Christine (*curtly*) Well this isn't a shelter for the homeless.

Pratt smiles, takes a stroll around the room, looking everywhere. Christine has to struggle with herself not to look at him

Pratt I should say not. Very nice. Bit of a come down of course. Not the lap of luxury as you might say. But then, all good things come to an end, I suppose. (*Pratt moves towards the steps*) I'll give you a hand with those.

Pratt takes one of the curtains from her and some plastic hooks

(*After a pause*) You looked as though you were expecting someone when I came to the door.
Christine (*after a pause*) I was.
Pratt Who?
Christine (*with contemptuous deliberation*) The furniture people. With a three-piece suite. Reduced, if you want to know the facts, from a hundred and twelve pounds to eighty-four. In tangerine cirrus. Is that all right by you?
Pratt (*after a pause*) It's not my favourite colour.
Christine (*angrily*) Look!
Pratt (*mildly*) Yes?
Christine Do you have any business here?
Pratt Yes.
Christine What?
Pratt I'm looking for the money.
Christine (*challenging him*) And you think it's here?
Pratt (*apologetically*) It might be.
Christine (*scornfully*) Where?
Pratt In that parcel you just brought in.

Christine imperceptibly halts in her turn away from Pratt as she suddenly realizes where the parcel to which Pratt is referring, is—in the cupboard

Christine It's more curtains, that's all.

Pratt (*with a smile*) That's just what I thought you'd say.

Christine (*impatiently*) John Lewis. Remnants in a sale. Do you want to see the receipt?

Pratt (*after a pause*) I'd rather see the parcel.

Christine (*angrily*) Well you can't. (*With pleading weariness now*) Do you think, if I had the money or knew where it was, I'd come to live in a place like this?

Pratt thinks about it

Pratt (*calmly*) Yes, I do. You must think like Jack does by now. I bet you always say to yourself, what would Jack tell me to do? And do you know what he'd tell you?

Christine (*shortly*) Yes. To crash these bloody steps over your head.

Pratt clicks his tongue disapprovingly

Pratt No, no, Jack was never like that. Violent, yes. But it was a deep, ultimate kind of violence he always had. You're just being aggressive and that's superficial, unthinking. No, Jack would have said—(*thinking it out*)—move into a modest little flat somewhere in the Willesden area. That way no-one will ever think you've got money. (*Reflecting*) Though mind you, property in Willesden fetches a price these days. How much did they sting you for this, Christine?

Christine I'll give you an introduction to the estate agents.

Pratt I've already met them. (*As Christine stares at him*) Just routine. Who your neighbours are, that kind of thing.

Christine I wouldn't know.

Pratt There's a Mr Freeman one side. In the jewellery trade apparently. Spends most of his time abroad. And a Miss Clitheroe. Works for *The Economist*. They sound respectable enough. (*Pause*) What's in the parcel, Christine?

Christine continues to ignore him, carries on with her work

Christine You won't find half a million. I'll tell you that.

Pratt I know. It wouldn't fit. But you'd get a fair bit in.

Christine (*with sarcasm*) Oh, don't bother about my little cut. Go for the jackpot. I had a new bed delivered yesterday. Why don't you take a look? Perhaps it's all stuffed in the mattress?

Pratt (*regretfully*) No. It came straight from the manufacturers. I checked. Nice bed. Comfortable. But a three foot single! You intend to stay faithful to his memory, I see. Touching.

Pratt is threading a hook into a curtain. Christine snatches the curtain away from him angrily

Christine You've gone too far now. I'm warning you, lay off. Or I'll make a laughing stock of you the way Jack always did. Wouldn't look too good in the newspapers, would it? Ex-Superintendent Pratt arrested.

Pratt looks at her, spreads his hands in innocence

Pratt For what?

Christine Trespass, for a start.

Pratt I'm willing to leave. (*Pratt makes a move as though to the door. He picks up Christine's coat, and asks politely*) Shall I hang this up for you? (*He goes towards the cupboard*)

Christine (*getting to the cupboard before him and snatching the coat*) No! And don't try and soft talk your way out of it. You just try and explain to the Commissioner—because that's who I'll complain to—what right you've got to go around snooping and questioning about that money.

Pratt I've already spoken to him.

Christine All pals together, eh? Well, I'll write to my M.P.

Pratt (*coolly*) You can take it to the House of Lords, Christine, if you like. I've got every right. I'm a private investigator.

Christine For yourself. (*She puts the coat back on the chair*)

Pratt No. For the insurance company's assessors. Here, if you don't believe me—my card.

Pratt steps forward, taking a card from his breast pocket. He offers it to Christine who ignores it. Pratt smiles, places it carefully on the top of the steps

Just a little part time job. We don't get much pension, you know. But it does give me a legal entitlement to pursue—well, my hobby you might say. I'm surprised you doubted me, Christine. I'd never break the law. You ask Jack.

Christine stares at him with quick suspicion

Sorry. Slip of the tongue. I find it hard to realize he's gone.

Christine still stares

What's the matter? Have I upset you?

Christine covers her fear with curtness

Christine All right. So you're entitled to ask questions. And I'm entitled to refuse to answer them.

Pratt answers with total reasonableness and begins to take a little stroll around the room as he answers, moving dangerously close to the cupboard. Christine tries to get on with her work but she cannot help but watch Pratt as he moves, quite casually, first near the cupboard—even to the extent of leaning on it—then away from it

Pratt Of course you are. There's nothing I can do about it, except put in a report to that effect. Then it's up to the company. Of course if they want to take further action, it's up to them. And no doubt they'll be guided by my report. All I'm saying is: think first, Christine, before you just throw me out. That's what Jack would have said, isn't it? Am I right? Think first.

Christine There's nothing to think about. I don't know where the money is and I've told you a hundred times.

Pratt Ah, that was in my official capacity.

Pratt's constant proximity to the cupboard is beginning to fray Christine's nerves. She yells at him

Christine If I don't know, I don't know. Can't you get that into your thick skull?

Pratt lifts his eyebrows in mute reproach at this outburst

Pratt Right. I'll go then. (*Pause*) If I could have a glance at that parcel.

Christine's nerve breaks. She moves towards Pratt, blocking him from entry to the cupboard

Christine No you bloody well can't. So get out! (*She opens the room door*)

Simultaneously Pratt suddenly takes a quick step towards the cupboard, and opens the door. Christine turns at the sound, gasps. The cupboard is empty—except for the parcel. Christine's back is to the audience. She is staring at the cupboard

Pratt (*with mock innocence*) Sorry. Wrong door. Oh, look. There's the parcel. (*He frowns as he looks at Christine*) What's the matter? You look as though you've seen a ghost.

Christine turns her back on Pratt so as not to give more of her shock away, Pratt looks from her to the parcel and back to her. His face reflects all his suspicions. He had not really expected to find anything in the parcel but now he is not sure. Why is Christine so tensed up about it? He picks up the parcel with a quick glance at Christine. It is a long moment of silence. Christine too has to work things out. She knows she must cover up that moment of shock. She is at the same time asking herself where Jack has disappeared to, and how should she play it now with Pratt

Christine I'm just—fed up that's all. I can't take any more of it. Being followed everywhere. The questioning. Can't you see that?

Pratt Yes. I'm sorry.

But Pratt makes no move. Christine turns, looks at him, then nods towards the parcel

Christine Go on. Open it. And then get out and leave me alone. Please.

Pratt looks at her, warily. But he takes her at her word, slides down the string, opens it, all the time looking at Christine. Pratt slides his hand inside the parcel and fumbles around. Then his whole body freezes for a moment. Both of them are totally still: a tableau

Pratt Nice. John Lewis's, did you say?

Christine Yes.

Pratt I could do with some new curtains.

Christine Satisfied?

Pratt (*after a pause*) For now.

Christine (*wearily*) You're not going to keep on.

Pratt (*after a pause*) I've got to.

Christine Why?

Pratt smiles thinly at her. He carefully repacks the parcel, puts it back in the cupboard, exactly as he found it. Christine watches every movement. Pratt closes the cupboard door—pauses

Pratt Don't be so anxious to get rid of me, Christine. There might come a time when you'd be glad to have me by your side.

Christine struggles to find a flash of spirit

Christine Maybe. If I sat next to you in a plane. About to crash.
Pratt (*in a hard tone*) I'm serious. (*He reverts to his old, always slightly mocking tone*) You know—Jack always thought ahead. But he always thought ahead on the premise that he'd be there. It's different now.
Christine How?
Pratt (*in a hard tone again*) I mean you haven't got him to protect you.
Christine I can look after myself.
Pratt (*with a shrug*) There's some bad characters around.
Christine Like?
Pratt Like Frenchy Highams.

Pratt has delivered the line seriously, and for effect. Christine is coming back to normal now, having got over that first shock. She twists her lips in contempt

Christine That slag.
Pratt That's not you talking, Christine. It's Jack. Frenchy may have been a slag compared with him but now that Jack's gone, Frenchy is top man. He always has been, south of the river. Now the word is, he wants Jack's manor.
Christine He can have it.
Pratt Don't be so quick to give it away. For men like Highams and Jack, crime is business. And this is a takeover.

Pratt pauses, watching Christine carefully the whole time. Pratt is now secretly bewildered by the sudden return of Christine's toughness, just when he thought he had broken her down. He must try once more—to break her down

He'll want to take over the assets of the business as well.
Christine Well I'm not one of them.
Pratt The money is.
Christine (*with exasperation*) For Christ's sake, how many times do I have to tell you . . .?
Pratt (*in a very hard tone*) Don't tell me. Tell Frenchy.
Christine (*confronting him*) Are you trying to scare me?
Pratt I'm just telling you that his interrogations would be less gentlemanly than mine. My ex-mob found a feller in a garage the other week, in Streatham. A grass. They'd nailed him to the rafters.

Pratt demonstrates. Christine shudders

Rough. (*Seeing that Christine is turned away from him, he takes a glove from his coat pocket and kicks it under a chair*)

Christine (*in a tough voice*) If I met Frenchy Highams . . .

Christine breaks off, thinking that in fact, without Jack, she would not know what to do. Pratt breaks in on her pause, quickly

Pratt What would you do? Call the police? Jack would turn in his grave.

Christine, half turning away, turns back on him furiously. Pratt continues quickly, raising a hand in peace

No offence. Really. (*With a change of tone*) I'm serious, Christine. So long as I'm around, you're safe. I may not be a top jack any more but I still have my connections, on both sides of the fence. Even Highams is not going to take any liberties with me.

Christine Nor with me.

Pratt Don't be too sure.

Christine What is this? Another part time job? The protection racket?

Pratt Be serious, Christine. Your life's in danger. You were under police surveillance until last Thursday. And then the case was closed, officially. By now, they must know that. And I reckon they would have moved. Only I've been watching you. They know that, too. Because they've been watching me. (*He smiles*) It's cat and mouse, Christine. And you're the mouse.

Christine is genuinely shaken by Pratt

Christine It's not fair. I don't know where that money is. I don't. I know you think I'm pretending, but it's true. Jack never told me. He wouldn't tell me.

Pratt I believe you. But will Frenchy Highams?

Christine (*with despair*) What the hell can I do? Run away?

Pratt They'll find you. (*Pause*) I'd find you.

Christine I thought you said you believed me?

Pratt I do. I believe you don't know where the money is. I believe Jack never told you. (*With sudden urgency*) But if you work with me, Christine —with what you know and what I know—we might be able to find it. And there's a ten per cent reward! More than fifty thousand pounds!

Christine (*with an irritable shrug*) How could I claim a reward?

Pratt Don't forget I work for the company. Maybe I could fix it.

Christine (*after a pause*) Why should you do that?

Pratt (*with vehemence*) Don't you see? It wraps up the case for me. Right now, Jack's still laughing in his grave . . .

Christine shudders, turns away. Pratt makes no apology

Look, forget the past, it's over and done with. Jack's dead. Yes, all right, it hurts, but he's dead. Face up to it. You'll never see him again. You might as well forget him. Start a new life somewhere. In the sun. You'd like that. Spain. I went to the Costa Brava last year. It's lovely. Like Blackpool. But warm. Come on, Christine, what do you say? Think!

Christine (*after a pause*) Is that a proposition?

Pratt (*after a pause*) It could be.

Christine Are you serious?

Pratt Take it which way you like. If you want to laugh, laugh. Maybe a change from what you've always known.

Christine How do you know what my life's been like?

Pratt I know more about you than you think. I found out. I had to. It was all part of knowing about Jack. (*He circles Christine, watching her*) Born in the Gorbals, one of those new housing estates. But still a slum. Slum people are slum people wherever you put them.

Christine Is that so?

Pratt Kept yourself pretty straight, didn't you? Travelled down to Middlesbrough, became a waitress for a while. Then a hostess in a night club. Better class waitress, you might say.

Christine It paid well. And I never did any whoring.

Pratt I never said you did. I think you showed great strength of character. It was harder not to be a whore than to be one, I'll bet. Maybe that's why you got into trouble with the law. Grievous bodily harm. Breaking a bottle over a customer's head.

Christine He deserved it.

Pratt That's what the judge thought. Can't complain about British justice, can you?

Christine (*with bitterness*) The police didn't have to bring the charge in the first place.

Pratt Just doing their job. Moved to another night club after that. Did a bit of stripping and dancing too. You might have had a theatrical career opening for you, Christine. But then you met Jack.

Christine Was that against the law?

Pratt No. Not until you became his accomplice.

Christine Prove it! Why should I tell you? I've already turned down three thousand quid from one Sunday paper.

Pratt Yes, I know. Do you know how much the same paper offered me? Four hundred! Jack could have named his own price.

Christine Jealous?

Pratt Of Jack? His success? His glory? His life style? Yes. Who wouldn't be? He had everything, didn't he? Beautiful wife. Nice home. All the money in the world. A natural charm. Everyone fell for Jack, men and women alike.

Christine What do you mean by that?

Pratt I'm not saying he's a poof.

Christine What then? That he had other women?

Pratt (*offhand*) Oh Christine! I'm sorry. I thought you knew.

Christine No, I don't. Tell me.

Pratt What for? I thought you wanted to keep his memory perfect and untouched?

Christine I know you want to smirch it.

The Lights start to fade slowly

Pratt I just talk facts, Christine. I'm thick, aren't I? It's all someone like me can go on. Facts. You think what you like. I'm telling you, Jack was no bloody hero. He had his weaknesses like anybody else. And if you never saw them, you were the one that was blind.

Christine (*challengingly*) All right. Tell me the facts.

Pratt Oh no. I've got something you want to know. You've got something I want to know. Let's trade.

Christine Trade what? Gossip? Tittle tattle?

Pratt Facts.

Christine Get stuffed.

Pratt (*with a shrug*) If you want to be like that . . .

Christine I do. Now get out.

Pratt All right. But think about it.

Christine There's nothing to think about. If Jack kept a dozen whores, I'd still fancy him more than I could you. Jack's got . . .

Christine breaks off, realizing she is talking in the present tense. Pratt bores in, quickly

Pratt (*in a hard tone*) He's got nothing, Christine. He's dead. (*He moves towards the door but pauses to hand Christine a card*) My card. If you change your mind.

Christine takes the card

Christine I won't.

She tears up the card. Pratt shrugs. He moves to the door, but pauses there to make sure he has her attention

Pratt Frenchy Highams might change it for you.

Pratt goes out. The front door closes

Christine goes to the window and looks out, then opens the cupboard door

Jack is standing in the cupboard, holding the champagne bottle and a revolver

Christine (*furiously*) Do you have to keep scaring the bloody life out of me?

Jack (*coming out of the cupboard*) What an old git! I'm sorry. I thought I explained about the cupboard. Mick built it. He's very handy, you know. (*He demonstrates that the back of the cupboard is hinged*)

Christine turns her back on him. Jack closes the cupboard door

Christine He's not the only one, it seems.

Jack What? Here, you're not taking a blind bit of notice of old Pratty, are you? That's all technique. (*He puts the bottle and revolver on a chair*)

Christine (*coldly*) I'm sure.

Jack Course it is. Here, don't believe me, ask him to show you the Metropolitan training manual—Page eighteen, Manipulation of Suspects. If it was the other way round, he'd be saying the same to me about you.

Christine (*turning to confront him*) All right, tell me the truth then, God's honest truth. There's never been anyone else?

Jack Well there's been a few birds fancy me, I don't deny it. I can't help it. It's my charisma.

Christine (*turning away again*) I'd like to chop your bloody charisma off.

Jack Oh, don't be like that. Come on ... (*He tries to caress her but Christine starts away from him, and now he is offended*) I suppose you've never had a few geysers after you?

Christine (*defiantly*) Quite a few.

Jack And you never ever encouraged them, I suppose? Never ever gave them the old come on?

Christine No.

Jack Bloody liar.

Christine (*wheeling*) You're the bloody liar.

Jack pauses deliberately so that the loudness of her shout almost echoes in the small, empty room

Jack (*suddenly very quiet, menacing*) That's right. Tell the whole world you've got someone here.

Christine (*after a pause, quietly*) I'm sorry.

Jack Don't you see what I mean? You're acting just the way he wants you to. It's all a game we're playing, and he's using you. He's really twisted you up. I bet if you knew where that money was, you'd tell him —just to get back at me.

Christine (*starting to unpack the tea-chest*) I suppose that's why you never told me where it was hidden?

Jack That's one of the reasons, yes.

Christine And what are the others? Joan and Evelyn, to name two?

Jack Oh for Christ's sake, I told you what he was after. I told you!

Christine Who's shouting now?

Jack (*quieter*) Look. One. The best way to act is to believe what you're acting. And if you don't know, you can't tell them.

Christine One. (*She takes a brush and comb from the chest to the bedroom and returns*)

Jack (*refusing to be riled*) Two. Now I never mentioned Frenchy Highams or any of the other villains either. But don't think it didn't cross my mind that they would think aye, aye, let's have a little nibble at Christine then.

Christine Oh, you must have been very worried. (*She takes a mirror from the chest to the bedroom and returns*)

Jack (*meaning it*) I'm not kidding, if you don't give up, I'm going to belt you right across the room. What do you think I had you move in here for, you silly cow? Now if you want to think I'm a bit stupid, that is stupid, fetching you right next door to the gaff where I'm hiding out. I did it to make sure that if you did have any unwelcome callers, inconvenient though it might be, I'd be here to deal with them.

Christine You've got it all worked out, haven't you?

Jack (*modestly*) That's what it's all about.

Christine (*increasing the level of her sarcasm*) How were you going to get rid of Frenchy Highams? Through the disposal unit in the kitchen, I suppose.

Jack Now don't be silly. (*Thoughtfully*) There's a rubbish chute on the landing. Fit him lovely. The rubbish bins downstairs are about this high. (*He demonstrates, above his head*) He'd grind up a treat on the old dustcart.

Christine Oh, Jack. . . .

She shudders away from him and then bursts into tears. Jack moves to comfort her

Jack Oh, come on—see, you've upset yourself? I told you. Honestly, that bastard Pratty. I'd like to kick him right in the cobblers, honest I would. Eh. . . I know what this is all about. He's put you in this agonizing dilemma, ain't he? Me or him?

Christine starts to laugh through her tears

Well, I understand, dear. I mean, if you fancy him . . .

Christine Oh, Jack, you know he gives me the creeps.

Jack He'd do well in them horror films, wouldn't he? (*He hunches himself up*) The monster of New Scotland Yard. (*As she recovers*) Now—do you want to know where the money is?

Christine No.

Jack I'll tell you.

Christine No. Honestly. I don't want to know.

Jack You believe me then?

Christine I don't know about believing you—(*with a flash of bitterness*)—to tell you the truth, I hate the bloody money.

Jack Eh?

Christine All I want is you, Jack. Can't you see that? The money doesn't matter.

Jack Yes. I know. But it's nice to have, isn't it?

Christine I'm not so sure about that. It's going to be with us all our lives.

Jack I hope so. Earning interest, Keeping us in comfort.

Christine Or in fear.

Jack (*warningly*) Now—you're starting again.

Christine (*clinging to him*) I just want to leave now, Jack. Oh, can't we?

Jack You know we can't. I explained. It's not long now. And then we'll be together. For good.

Christine That's what I want, Jack.

Jack That's what I want, Chris. A new name. New life. No more running, hiding. No more excitement like a ball of lead in my stomach. I always made a laugh of it but if you knew how shit scared I was sometimes . . .

Christine I did know. I always knew.

Jack It'll be different now. But don't sneer at the money. That's our passport. Here, talking about leaving—you'll have to go.

Christine (*disappointed*) Oh, Jack . . .

Jack Well you can't stay here. Old Pratty might be hanging about waiting to see you go. (*He imitates a P.C. on the beat*) Evening, all.

Christine does not smile. She is offended

Christine All right. (*She starts to move towards the door*)

Jack Where're you going?

Christine You told me to go.

Jack Yes. After.

Christine (*coquettishly*) After what?

Jack What do you think? Listen, I've been cooped up in that bug hole next door for five weeks all on my tod. Oh it's very comfortable, all mod cons, just bloody lonely that's all. I tell you, the bloke on the radio says good morning, I answer him back I'm so bloody grateful for someone to talk to.

Christine (*seriously*) How do you think it's been for me?

Jack Well maybe—but at least you'd had some sort of contact with reality. I asked Mick to leave me some good books, help pass the time away. What did I find? Half a dozen paper backs, all crime stories, and a load of nude magazines. I've got the choice of being dead bored, or dead randy.

Christine Well I'm here now.

Jack (*kissing her*) Did you lock the door?

Christine Yes.

Jack (*kissing her*) You're sure?

Christine I double locked it.

They kiss then break

Jack Good. Only there's a lot of villains about. You've got to be careful. Here, we can open that bubbly now. That's good for anniversaries. It's Taittinger—the best.

Christine Anniversary? That was last March.

Jack I knew you didn't remember. Our first time. In that little sports car I had.

Christine (*with a giggle*) I don't know how we did it.

Jack You needed to be a contortionist, didn't you? I can still remember that bloody steering wheel.

Christine I still remember how it felt when you sat on the hooter.

Jack It was about the only time I was ever really scared about being nicked. The bloody horn was blaring out——

Christine —and we couldn't untangle ourselves.

Jack I drove off like a bat out of hell. If I'd been nicked for speeding, I'd have looked a right burke. With no trousers. (*A pause*) It was a bit of a flop, wasn't it?

Christine (*tenderly*) We made up for it later. (*She takes the champagne*)

Jack Here! Where are you going with that champagne?

She moves towards the bedroom door, pauses to stare challengingly at Jack

Christine Are you coming? Or do I have to drag you in?

Christine exits into the bedroom, with the champagne

Jack Oh, you are so crude—just a minute . . .

Jack picks up two glasses from the chest and follows her into the bedroom. The dialogue continues in the bedroom

(*Off*) Here, steady. You'll find yourself in the Guinness Book of Records. Fastest strip tease in the West. Get 'em off!

Pratt enters from the cupboard and, while the dialogue continues in the bedroom, he aims his pistol through the bedroom door, but a laugh from Christine makes him change his mind. He picks up Jack's revolver from the chair, empties the bullets into his pocket and replaces the revolver on the chair. He then retrieves his glove from under the other chair and quietly exits into the cupboard, shutting the door behind him

Christine (*off*) And you call me crude! Are you going to pour that champagne or not?
Jack (*off*) Give us a chance. I can't get the cork out. I keep getting distracted.

Sound of a pop as the cork flies

Christine (*off*) Where are the glasses?
Jack (*off*) There they are. Quick! We're wasting it. There.
Christine (*off*) Lovely!
Jack (*off*) Just like you.
Christine (*off*) Well let me drink it then.
Jack (*off*) No. I've changed my mind.
Christine (*off*) No, Jack, don't!
Jack (*off*) Why do you always say no when you mean yes?
Christine (*off*) I don't. Oh, Jack!
Jack (*off*) Shut up!
Christine (*off*) Ooooh Jack . . .

The love scene in the bedroom reaches a climax as Pratt exits into the cupboard, and—

the CURTAIN *falls*

SCENE 2

A cellar

When the CURTAIN *rises it is very dark on stage. The Lights come up very slowly, imperceptibly, almost. We become aware of a shape in the centre of the stage, and gradually see that it is Jack. He is lying huddled on the floor, secured by handcuffs which are chained to a ring in the floor. The chain, which is about three feet long, has been shortened to about six inches by a padlock through two links. The Lights come up further and it is revealed that the setting is a cellar with a single door and steps leading down*

Two bolts are heard to slide, and the door opens. Pratt enters, fumbles for the light switch, then turns it on. A single unshaded bulb is illuminated. Pratt carries a thermos and a brandy flask. He moves to Jack and looks down at him. Jack moves and Pratt quickly backs. He shuts the door and smiles in a jocular fashion at Jack

Pratt All right, boy?

Jack lies motionless. Pratt comes down the steps. Pratt circles him cautiously, making absolutely sure that Jack is held fast, before approaching

Pratt Sleep well? Uncomfortable? Cold? Hungry? Thirsty?

Pratt moves away to pick up two orange boxes, returns and arranges them as two stools, on either side of Jack

You try anything and I'll chain you up like an animal. All right?

Jack just glowers at him

Jack What d'you call this, then?

Pratt I don't know, do I? I'm an old pratt, remember? I mean, I'm surprised to find you here. What happened to the old Houdini bit?

Jack That's all right, Pratty. I'll always beat you.

Pratt Well, we'll see. I mean, it's a bit different from the last time, isn't it? The miraculous escape from stupid old Pratt. I knew there was a bit of bribery in the background there.

Jack Clever you.

Pratt But this time, it's just you and me. In a vacuum like. So this time we're putting it to the test properly.

Jack Oh yes. Very fair. Why don't you blindfold me as well?

Pratt Because I want to see your eyes, Jack, that's why.

Pratt's intensity is chilling. But Jack meets his gaze. There is still a hint of contempt in his voice

Jack You won't see me get frightened of you, mate.

Pratt We'll see. (*He throws a key to Jack*)

Jack unlocks the padlock and rises slowly and painfully to the full extent of the chain. There is a moment of challenge between them. Then Jack seems to shrug off his tenseness, his fear perhaps. He grins across at Pratt. This is the old confident Jack, or so it seems. He could be just putting on an act to distract Pratt in a war of nerves

Jack All right, love. What's it all about then?

Pratt I just wanted to have a little talk with you.

Jack We could have had that when you found me. Or in the comfort of your centrally heated office with its nice potted palms.

Pratt Ah, no. It's against the rules, you see.

Jack I forgot. You retired. I thought you had anyway.

Pratt I've still got common law powers. It's not that. It's arresting a dead man, you see. It's not allowed.

Jack A small technicality like that wouldn't bother you.

Pratt I expect I could get around it.

Jack I'm sure you could. Why don't you?

Pratt Perhaps I don't want to.

Jack I don't have what they call a giant intellect, Pratty, but I worked that out for myself. Why don't you want to?

Pratt I'll tell you. In my own good time.

Jack Please yourself. I'd have thought you were bursting to tell me. (*He grins at Pratt, almost with a kind of affection*) Come on, you know you're dying to.

Pratt is equally frank and intimate in his reply. The conversation might be between two close friends

Pratt No. Really. When you've wanted something for a long time, and you get it, you don't want to gobble it all up. You want to savour it. Relish it. You know what I mean.

Jack Well I know. But wouldn't you like to make a meal of it sitting by a plate glass window, like? With the hungry public staring in and saying look, there he is, the great Pratt, as he likes to think of himself, or the big Pratt, as Jack Robin used to call him. But he's got Jack served up on a plate now.

Pratt considers the point

Pratt That would be very tempting. I must admit. In fact that was, you might say, my ambition at one time. But then you spoiled that for me.

Jack I spoiled it for you more than once.

Pratt I'm not digging up past history. I mean when you had your nasty accident.

Jack Because you wrote me off? You couldn't have got much satisfaction out of that. I mean, how many people die in road crashes every day? Twenty, twenty-five? Just another figure in the statistics, mate.

Pratt I never said it was very satisfactory.

Jack Mind you, I thought you handled the P.R. bit quite well. Quite gave the impression that you single-handed punctured the tyres of the car, didn't you? Until the inquest, anyway.

Pratt I got you. I wrote you off. That was what mattered to me. But don't think I was hoodwinked, Jack. I don't say I knew what was going on but I knew something was. When I walked into that surgery. When your coffin was lowered into that grave, Jack, it didn't feel right. It was instinctive. You know? Like it is with a marriage after years and years, happy or unhappy. Like when my wife died. I'm not saying we got on all that well. My fault, I suppose, I always worked too hard. Obsessional, that's always been my trouble. But when her coffin moved through those trap doors—she always wanted to be cremated, had it in her will even, when that coffin disappeared—they do it very nicely, recorded organ music, choir, everything—I knew she was gone, it was all over because we were close, you see, not in any great loving way, I'm not pretending that, but years of thinking about a person—thinking about what they're thinking—it's a special kind of intimacy. Do you know what I mean,

Jack? For me, you were never gone. And I'm not superstitious. I didn't think you were haunting me. I knew that something was wrong and once I knew that, I knew everything—well nearly everything. I just had to work it out, that's all. It all worked for you, Jack, and it all worked against you. Yes, I let you have your little joke. Yes, I did what you wanted me to do. I kept quiet. I retired. But I never gave up Jack. I just watched and waited, watched and waited. But it was a clever scheme, I'll give you that.

Jack Don't give anything away, will you? I've pulled a few strokes, Pratty, as you know, but that was my greatest, you must admit. And you helped me. (*He leans forward and speaks with apparent sincerity*) No, seriously, guv'nor. I'm grateful for that. I mean it.

Pratt looks at him, amused

Pratt Now I wonder what you mean by that?

Jack smiles but there is a tenseness about him. We hear the slight edge of it in his voice

Jack Well, you tell me what you're playing at and I might make a proposition.

Pratt Do you think, seriously, that I'd consider any proposition from you?

Jack's nerve suddenly falters, enough to make him snap

Jack Well if you're just after the glory, what the hell did you drag me to this hole for?

Pratt I said, I'll tell you, but you've got to be patient.

Jack Look, if you're playing the straight copper part bit, then I know my rights, mate, and you can't hold me here.

Pratt (*sharply*) You haven't got any rights, Jack. You're dead. That's the beauty of it, you see. Your greatest stroke, definitely. You really put it over poor old Pratty. But you put it over everyone else as well. And that way, you left me with all the cards in my hand. The stroke misfired, Jack. You're dead. (*He addresses him with a quiet sadism*) You might say we're the only two people left in the world. In your world.

Jack Oh no we're not. There's still Christine.

Pratt Christine? Well, what's she going to do when she gets back to the flat and finds you've scarpered? Go and tell the police that you're alive, but missing? The only way she could prove that is by telling them that you murdered Adcock. And I'll tell you something about your wife, Jack, though I suppose you don't need me to tell you. She's a very sensual person. Am I right? You've got a big thing between you, haven't you. Surprised you had time for the champagne. She couldn't stand being parted from you for life.

Jack (*explosively*) She's not going to stand being parted from me anyway. She'd rather know if I was dead.

Pratt Ah. That depends. On the conclusions she draws. If certain evidence were planted, say, suggesting that you might have gone off for some reason, possibly with another woman . . .

Jack leaps up from his seat and drags the full length of his tie towards Pratt, who is just out of reach

Jack You're a crooked bastard, Pratt, just like every other bloody copper. . .

Pratt clicks his tongue loudly in reproof

Pratt Now you're wrong, Jack, and you'll have to take that back. I did forty-three years in the force and never took a backhander once. (*Pause*) And I've had pressure put on me from both sides, mate, before now, but I always did my duty, laugh at the idea if you like. (*He walks away from Jack, keeping in a circle, on the periphery of the length of the tie*) But the day they accepted you as officially dead, Jack, I resigned from the force. I retired. They gave me a nice parting present. I'll show it to you sometime. A clock.

Jack You know what you can do with that.

Pratt It's not like you to be so rude, Jack. What is it? Are you getting nervous?

Jack trails his bonds back to the orange box, sits down. He bows his head wearily

Jack Why don't we come to the point, eh?

Pratt I'm in no hurry. I've got all the time in the world.

Jack raises his head to look at Pratt directly. He is deadly serious now

Jack How much time have I got?

Pratt Don't rush me. I'm a man of leisure now.

Jack Is this your new hobby? Tormenting people? I thought you were going to have a go at the bees? What's the matter, do they sting back?

Pratt (*suddenly sharp*) What about the years you spent tormenting me?

Jack Oh for Christ's sake, it was nothing personal.

Pratt It was personal to me. It might have been any old butt to you.

Jack All right, I'm sorry.

Pratt You will be, Jack. Very sorry.

Jack stares across at Pratt. Jack is unafraid now, hard

Jack I'm not finished yet, you know. So long as my mind's ticking, you'll never be safe. I can still outwit you, Pratty.

Pratt That's fair enough. If you can.

Jack I don't mind you pulling me in here, getting a bit of your own back. But if you're really going to try pulling that one on Christine, I'll murder you, mate.

Pratt I find your reaction very interesting. To Christine I mean. I wasn't sure she'd ever fall for that but I see you've got your doubts. Bit on the jealous side, is she? Suspects you of going for a bit of spare now and then? Well—she might want to pay you back in your own coin.

Jack refuses to let himself get rattled

Jack We've already had that out, mate. She knows your game. I told her. I heard you through the cupboard. It was pathetic. We had a right giggle about you afterwards. I don't know why you always go on about people laughing at you, Pratty. You are laughable. You're a bloody clown.

Pratt (*after a long pause*) We'll see. Let's have our little talk now, shall we, Jack!

Jack watches him. There is an intentness about Jack now. He is a coiled man, waiting for a chance to strike

Jack All right.

Pratt Where shall we begin?

Jack I suppose you can tell me how you knew, for a start.

Pratt (*casually*) Oh, when Adcock disappeared. I mean it was too much, wasn't it? Boat overturned. Body missing. I wasn't going to swallow that.

Jack So why didn't you investigate?

Pratt What was I going to do? Have you exhumed. Make myself a laughing stock? You know, Jack. You know bloody well why. That was the way you set it up.

Jack Simple psychology, weren't it?

Pratt You've always been a bit of a psychologist, Jack.

Jack I'm glad you appreciate it.

Pratt Well, I studied the subject myself. Not in any depth, mind.

Jack Just the odd article in *Reader's Digest*?

Pratt Are you taking the mick?

Jack Well, you do ask for it. I mean, you're not exactly the intellectual type, are you? Admit it.

Pratt I outsmarted you, Jack. I found you.

Jack Yeh. How?

Pratt (*bringing down a third beer-crate, and pouring coffee and brandy into the thermos cup*) Well almost by accident, really. I was just doing my job. My new job, I mean. Wondering whether Christine knew where that money was or not. That was why I called on her, in her new flat and I find her strangely tense, nervous. Why, I asked myself? (*He drinks*)

Jack And what did you answer yourself?

Pratt (*with a shrug*) For no reason, I said at first. Or for all the obvious reasons, and then I started asking myself other questions.

Jack I suppose no-one else will listen to you?

Pratt Like—why was I kept waiting two hours, outside Maison Charles?

Jack Well you've lost me. Why?

Pratt Because she was having a nice new hair-do, that's why.

Jack What's that got to do with it?

Pratt Perhaps she's expecting Jack to pay her a visit, I said.

Jack Well you were wrong. She didn't even know I was there.

Pratt No, but it was another clue, Jack, that you were alive. And what does it matter how I got there, I got there. I drove away and then came back, hung around a bit. I'd left a glove there, just as an excuse to call again. I nearly rang the door bell, Jack, and then I heard raised voices. It was a bad time to have an argument, Jack. You slipped up there. I knew no-one could have gone into that building. All I'd done was turn the car round in the street. So if no-one had gone in through the door, then they must have had some other form of entrance. So I paid a little visit to the next door flat, and since there was no-one there, Mr Freeman! I thought I'd just nip in, have a look.

Jack Yes. They call it breaking and entering.

Pratt Is that it? Why don't you report me, Jack? Oh but you can't. I keep forgetting. You have no real standing in society. Anyway, what does it matter, hey? I found you!

Jack By accident.

Pratt By persistence. Logical thought. I knew you were around somewhere. I'm not so stupid as some people think. I had to leave school at thirteen. You could leave in your fourteenth year, in those days, if you had a job to go to.

Jack Yes. Well, it was that Queen Victoria, she was like that. Where'd they put you? Up the chimneys or down the mines?

Pratt No. They put me as an apprentice bricklayer. But I wanted to be a copper even then. I went to evening school to get the education.

Jack That's the trouble with those places. They can't teach you much.

Pratt I got through all right.

Jack You should have stuck to bricklaying, mate. You might have become a millionaire property developer.

Pratt No. Not my style. Money's never come my way. It's always been a struggle. To keep decent, honest. Go on, laugh.

Jack No. Certainly not. My mum always said the same to me.

Pratt Pity you didn't take more notice.

Jack Do me a favour, Pratty. Stop preaching.

Pratt (*suddenly hard*) And you do me a favour—just stop taking the piss out of my name.

Jack (*in a mock injured tone*) All right. If it upsets you. But you shouldn't be so sensitive.

Pratt Well I am.

Jack Then you shouldn't be a copper.

Pratt I'm not, any more, which brings us back to the point, doesn't it?

Jack I don't know. I lost you. I thought you were talking about your life and hard times.

Pratt You've always had it easy, son.

Jack Now that's not true, Pratty, excuse me, I mean Mister Pratt. I was out grafting at thirteen too, in fact before that. I was only ten years old when I stripped the lead off my first roof.

Pratt That doesn't surprise me. I'm just surprised you started your career so conventionally.

Jack Yes. It was the police station roof, mind.

Pratt Very funny. I can never understand about you bright boys. You'd have probably done just as well going straight.

Jack Are we going to have a long chat about the class system and what's wrong with a capitalist society?

Pratt Not if you don't want to.

Jack I don't.

Pratt Right. (*He finishes his drink*) Anyway. There it was. I always suspected. But I had no proof. No-one else seemed to cotton on. So I let it go. Packed my things at the office. Made a little speech. Glass of sherry all round at the presentation. Very nice.

Jack You must have felt very proud.

Pratt No. Just eager. To find you.

Jack What for? The game was over.

Pratt Not for me, Jack. I wasn't giving up. You'd looked so far ahead, but not far enough. Like chess, you know. It's not enough to think one move ahead. You've got to think two, three, four. (*He moves close to Jack*)

Jack (*shortly*) I know. I can play.

Pratt moves away. They realize they have been close together for the first time. Pratt looks pleased at the quaintness of a thought that has occurred to him

Pratt We must have a game sometime. I suppose this is a kind of chess game, isn't it? That we're playing now.

Jack You won't win.

Pratt I'm well in front.

Jack You're not the type. You haven't got it. At best, you might force a draw.

Pratt I think you're judging on past performances, Jack. Remember, I had to stick to the rules then. You were the one allowed to break them.

Jack All right, now we're even.

Pratt The odds are better than that. Because I make the rules.

Jack (*wearily*) Oh come on, for Christ's sake, let's get to the point.

Pratt I've already got to it, I don't know about you. I'm telling you, Jack, you only thought about three moves ahead instead of four. You thought you'd stymied me but all you'd done, if you'll pardon me mixing my metaphors, was to move yourself into check.

Jack Oh, talk English.

Pratt (*patiently*) If the advantage to you was that I couldn't arrest you, because you were dead, the advantage to me was that I could. Well just take you, anyway.

Jack All right. You've got me. Now what?

Pratt Well, now this is an entirely private matter, do you see? Just between me and the ghost of Jack Robin. With, of course, the bonus I get from not being a police officer any more.

Jack Meaning?

Pratt The half a million, Jack. What else?

Jack I thought so. That was all on top, wasn't it, the bit about being an insurance investigator. A good cover. You're as crooked as the bleeding rest.

Pratt If you're casting aspersions on my former brother officers, well I can't answer for them. To the best of my knowledge, they're a decent lot. One or two go wrong, certainly. There's a lot of temptation, and especially from people like you. But I was always straight and, so far as I'm concerned, I still am. If you were alive now, my duty would be clear, even as a private citizen, but seeing you're not . . .

Jack (*crisply*) All right, save me the hypocrisy. If we're going to talk business, you can get these off for a start, and we'll talk in comfort.

Pratt We'll talk on my terms, Jack. They stay.

Jack For Christ's sake, what for? You've got a bloody gun in your pocket. You don't think I'd have come with you if you hadn't.

Pratt (*showing his gun*) I've got a license for it. Belonged to a shooting club for years. I wouldn't do anything that wasn't legal.

Jack All right, let's cut it short then. How much?

Pratt How much what?

Jack (*patiently*) What do you want for a cut? How much of the loot?

Pratt All of it.

Jack What?

Pratt Well naturally.

Jack You're bloody mad.

Pratt I've just retired, Jack.

Jack What the hell's that got to do with it?

Pratt The cost of living. It's rocketing. It hits people on fixed pensions.

Jack Well what d'you think you're going to do? Mix with the international bloody jet set?

Pratt I might.

Jack Come off it. You're not that far round the bend.

Pratt Well I have got my plans, to tell you the truth. But I don't see they're any of your business.

Jack Too bloody right they are, if it's on my money.

Pratt That's arguable, isn't it? You could say it never was your money in the first place.

Jack I'll tell you something else you could say. It'll never be yours.

Pratt Now that's a silly argument. You've got no option, have you?

Jack I could just say no.

Pratt You'd get very bored here, on your own. No light. Cold. Damp. I'm sure you'd rather be out of it.

Jack How long d'you think you could keep me?

Pratt For ever, if I wanted to.

Jack I'd get away somehow.

Pratt I don't think so. Without food or drink, you'd soon weaken. You'd be surprised.

Jack Are you saying you'd let me die?

Pratt Yes.

Jack That's murder.

Pratt Jack! You sound so shocked! And anyway, it's not. How can you murder a man who's already dead?

Jack Oh very clever.

Pratt That's what I thought.

Jack You bastard.

Pratt I don't think you appreciate, Jack, that I'm making you a very fair

offer. Admittedly, you lose your life savings, as it were, but that's
better than losing your life, isn't it?

Jack Very funny.

Pratt Just thought of it on the spur of the moment. On the other hand,
you've got your whole career ahead of you still. And look what a strong
position you're in. Your file marked deceased. Me out of the way. I'm
sure you'll be very successful. And you'll owe it all to me.

Pratt watches as Jack seems to think it over

Jack Bloody high price, though.

Pratt How could I ask less?

Jack You'd do yourself a favour. Look, I tell you what. We'll go halves.
And no hard feelings.

Pratt What do you take me for? You'll be after me, whatever happens.
So I need protection. That costs money.

Jack I'll give you my word . . .

Pratt (*packing up his flasks*) You can keep it. I'm not bargaining, Jack.
And I'm not going to argue the toss much longer either. You can have
twenty-four hours on your own to think about it. Tomorrow you might
not be so cocky.

*Pratt walks resolutely towards the steps. Jack moves quickly after him but is
pulled up by his halter*

Jack No, wait . . .

Pratt What for?

Jack Well let's talk about it.

Pratt There's nothing to talk about.

Jack (*desperately*) We've got to discuss the details.

Pratt shrugs, goes up the steps and switches off the light. Jack shouts at him

Don't leave me here on my own!

Pratt So long as it is just the details. (*He turns on the light and comes to the
handrail*)

Jack Yes. Right. (*He moves about, so far as the tie will allow him*) Where
is this place anyway?

Pratt What's that got to do with it? (*He puts the brandy flask in his pocket
and the thermos on the handrail*)

Jack I was just asking.

Pratt You weren't. You were conniving. You've trying to figure out what
the chances are of anyone finding you here.

Jack All right. Yes.

Pratt (*coming down*) Right. And since you're being honest about it, I'll
tell you. I'll lay all my cards on the table, Jack, and then you can make
your decision. (*He glances at his watch*) Three and a half minutes. Then
that's your lot. (*He sits down, looks around*) This place? It's the cellar
of my house. Funny sort of foundations, really. It's a kind of cellar
beneath a cellar. Didn't get much of a chance to see the house when

we came in, did you? Not a bad place. Detached. Victorian. Very solid.
Good thick walls. They don't make them like that any more.

Jack I only asked where we were. I wasn't thinking of buying the place.

Pratt I've had several good offers for it. It's a big garden you see. (*He
thinks*) Yes, they want to pull it down, build a row of terraced cottages.
(*Pause*) Town houses, they call them.

Jack (*sympathetically*) Spoil the look of the neighbourhood, would it?

Pratt I think so. I like it as it is. It's quiet, you know. You don't hear the
neighbours. And the neighbours don't hear you.

Jack refuses to be bludgeoned by the implicit menace in Pratt's tone

Jack That allows you to play your electric guitar, does it.

Pratt It enables me to keep you here, Jack.

*Pratt's voice is chilling. Almost inadvertently, Jack raises his eyes to the
ceiling, to assess his chances. Who is in the house? Anyone? Pratt follows his
glance and answers him, quite amicable again*

In the house? Just my old mother. She's eighty-three. Her room's on
the second floor. But she's stone deaf. The home help comes in, but not
till Monday. You'd be in a bad way by then. And I could put her off,
anyway.

Jack (*hoarsely*) It's not all that easy, you know. I mean someone would
find me some time . . .

Pratt Your body? Never. We've got a bit of an underground stream here.
Nuisance really. Knocks down the value of the property. If it wasn't
for that, they'd put up a block of flats instead of bloody town houses.
Make the whole thing worth while. More units of accommodation. Do
you see? Now and again, it swells up, floods the cellar. And there's a
sort of drainage pit. Leads down to it. The stream.

*Pratt lifts the trap door. The sound of a stream is heard. He closes the trap
again*

It's about two foot across.

Jack You've really got it worked out.

Pratt I'm not quite the fool you always took me for. (*He leans towards
Jack*) I'll tell you something. If you turn me down, I'm not going to
try and force you. In fact, I'll be kind of relieved. The money's going to
pose problems. I know that. It's something I'll be worrying about for
the rest of my life. But this, to leave you here. That'd be satisfaction,
Jack. You had a lot of laughs at my expense. I'd like to have the last
laugh myself, even if it was only with myself.

Jack (*shaken*) Christ, it was never that bad.

Pratt You wouldn't know. You were always one of the laughers. It's
different when you're being laughed at. So don't tempt me, Jack. I'm
trying to be sensible about this.

Jack (*after a pause*) All right. It's a deal.

Pratt Good. Where is it?

Jack Now wait a minute.

Pratt Forget it.

Jack (*panicking*) For Christ's sake! Don't be so touchy.

Pratt (*shouting back*) Are you going to tell me or not?

Jack Yes, I am. (*He collects himself*) But it is a deal. You let me go.

Pratt I told you.

Jack Well, I only want to protect myself.

Pratt Meaning what?

Jack Well you could top me and take the cash.

Pratt looks at him for a moment

Pratt (*reasonably*) That's true.

Jack Well let me go first.

Pratt laughs at him. Jack appeals desperately

Then we'll go together.

Pratt continues to laugh

I've got to have some guarantee.

Pratt You've got nothing, Jack. You just have to trust me. You've got no choice. (*He walks around Jack*) You see, you've told me the one thing I wanted to know. It occurred to me that picking it up might be a bit dodgy, it'd be well under guard.

Jack It is.

Pratt Ah, no. Or you wouldn't have said that I could top you and take the cash. If that's possible, then you've got no choice. Right?

Jack All right, I've got no choice. But you watch it because now your logic is playing against itself. If you're going to kill me anyway, then I'll see you go to buggery, you won't get that money.

Pratt Now why should I do that? I'm not a murderer.

Jack Well you've got all the bloody earmarks, mate. Christ, one minute you're telling me how you've got the dead needle to me and your ambition in life is to stuff me down the drain. And the next minute you're asking me to trust you!

Pratt Not asking you, Jack. Telling you. That you've got no choice.

Jack Well I don't see that.

Pratt All right, you've got a choice. To die a rich man or live a poor one.

Jack Or die a poor one. That's the third choice, the one you don't mention. And that's the one I worry about.

Pratt laughs at the retort

Pratt Now come on, Jack. You know I had to put the frighteners on you. (*He drinks from the brandy flask then puts it on the floor within reach of Jack*)

Jack makes a point of wiping the flask, then drinks

(*Sitting*) Let's just talk business now. Man to man. Right?

Jack Right. No messing about.

Pratt Good. Where is it?

Jack Just a minute. What's the plan?

Pratt What plan?

Jack To release me? If you've got it all worked out, mate, and I'm sure you have, you better have it worked out how I'm getting out. Or forget it. I'll die happy at least.

Pratt's smile fades. He switches it on again

Pratt All right, I'll tell you. But first of all, it's in cash, isn't it?

Jack Yes. All of it.

Pratt Good. Right. (*He takes a breath*) O.K. First of all, I fix you up here a bit more comfortable.

Jack What does that mean? Another six inches of chain?

Pratt Now be serious, boy. Then I'll go off to—where is it, roughly?

Jack In the country.

Pratt A few hours, there and back?

Jack Best part of a day.

Pratt Right. I'll take the old lady with me. She'll enjoy that.

Jack What is this, a bloody old age pensioner's outing? Why can't you leave her here?

Pratt You're not thinking ahead, Jack. I've got to get out before you, haven't I? And I can't disappear just like that. I've got to see she's all right first.

Jack (*angrily*) Look, how long d'you think . . . ?

Pratt Now don't worry about it. There're plenty of nursing homes. Hundreds of 'em. I've been studying them for years. The brochures, I mean. It's nowhere near Bournemouth, is it?

Jack No.

Pratt Pity, there's some good ones down there. Still, I can take my pick now that I'll have the money, I'll get her in somewhere en route. Don't you worry about it.

Jack Why should I worry? It's your mum you're getting rid of.

Pratt She'll be better off in a home.

Jack Yes I'm sure. But could I trouble you to worry about my welfare just for a minute?

Pratt I'll be thinking about you, Jack. All the time. (*He grins*) It's become a sort of habit over the years.

Jack That's nice.

Pratt Soon as I've got the money, I come straight back here. Upstairs I've got some strong sleeping pills.

Jack What the hell are they for? Or have you got an old aunt to get shot of as well?

Pratt No, no. They're for you. Just a couple. They'll soon send you off.

Jack I get it. What they call in the explosives game a delayed activating mechanism.

Pratt Right, You'll be out for about six, eight hours. And that's all the time I need. When you wake up, you'll be free to walk out of here. Right in your class, eh?

Jack considers the plan. Pratt watches him eagerly

Jack (*after a pause*) Well—I've got to hand it to you. Almost. Almost.

Pratt goes to Jack, holding his hand out for the flask

But I've still got one question, and it's an important one . . .
Pratt What?

Jack suddenly punches Pratt in the stomach, and, as Pratt drops to his knees, Jack lifts his arms over Pratt's head and starts to strangle him. Pratt tries to get away but finds himself being choked by the pressure of the manacles against his throat

Jack (*friendly*) It's this. What happens when I strangle you, then take the key to the cuffs out of your pocket?
Pratt (*choked*) I haven't got it on me. You ought to know better than that.
Jack All right then. Question two. What's to stop me murdering you, taking your gun, and shooting them off?

Jack squeezes at Pratt's throat. Pratt just finds voice to answer

Pratt Because there's no bullets in it.
Jack All right. Then in the words of the great Superintendent Pratt, otherwise known as the big pratt, we'll see!

Jack squeezes hard. Pratt chokes. Then Jack relaxes his grip, raises the manacles above Pratt's head, crashes them down. Pratt falls in a heap. Jack bends over him, goes through his pockets. He finds the revolver, but keeps on searching. Nothing. He flicks open the chamber of the revolver. It is empty. Jack drops the gun, sinks back on to the orange box. He slumps forward in total dejection

Pratt Well Jack? Give up?
Jack (*tonelessly*) I'll tell you.

Pratt stirs, drags himself to his feet. He is totally vindictive now

Pratt You'd better. (*Rising*) And remember. You're just relying on my bloody charity from now on. (*He picks up the gun and threatens to hit Jack*)
Jack Yes.
Pratt Right.
Jack (*after a pause*) You drive to Plymouth. Do you know it? You take the new bridge. Into Cornwall. Just a few miles in, you'll see it signposted. A place called Megarith. It's only a couple of dozen houses. Drive through it and then, as you leave, you'll see an old tin mine on the left. D'you know what a tin mine looks like?

Pratt threatens again to hit Jack

There'll be 'No Trespassing' signs all over the place. Take no notice. It's my property. (*Looking at Pratt*) There's only one shaft. It's not steep. You just walk down a slope. It's shored up with sort of wooden arches, about one every five yards. The seventh one is fake. I put it in specially.

It's a sort of hollow box with a steel girder inside it for support. The loot's inside.

Pratt Is that all?

Jack (*bitterly*) I don't know what you mean by all. For me it's everything.

Pratt (*after a pause*) All right, Jack I don't think you'd send me on a wild goose chase. (*He moves to the foot of the stairs*) You were clever, but I had your measure this time. Eh?

Jack (*bitterly*) Yeh. I should have strangled you when I had you. Your old mum would have soon squawked and they'd have found us both. But me, alive.

Pratt That's good thinking, Jack, but a bit late. You missed a trick there, didn't you? But never mind. You can't win 'em all.

Jack (*doggedly*) You won't beat me, Pratty. At worst I'll get a draw.

Pratt's eyes narrow

Pratt What do you mean by that? You got something else up your sleeve?

Jack stands up, kicking the box over. His voice is passionate

Jack I mean—you're coming back, aren't you?

Pratt's face clears

Pratt Oh, that. Well . . . (*He climbs the stairs. His smile is sour*) Like the big pratt always says: We'll see. Won't we? (*He goes up the steps, picks up the thermos, puts the light out, then turns in the doorway. He cannot resist a last malignant parting shot*) No, that's not fair, is it? Why should I leave you in suspense? No, I won't come back, Jack, and before I go, there's a little job I've been meaning to do for years. Brick up this cellar. It might stop the damp rising.

Jack (*scared*) Pratty, wait, listen . . .

Pratt chuckling, continues on his way out

Jack Pratty. Listen. For Christ's sake . . .
Pratt No, Jack. That's the end.

Pratt turns abruptly and goes out. There is the sound of two bolts being shot home, then of hurried footsteps retreating

Jack's eyes look up and his head moves as though tracing the path of the man upstairs. Jack screams after him, as the Lights start to fade

Jack Pratty, come back! Pratt. Mister Pratt! For Christ's sake, don't be a fool. Listen to me. You'll be sorry. (*His fear suddenly turns to rage*) All right, you bastard, don't. I'll get you yet, Pratty. You'll never beat me. (*He falls to his knees and sobs aloud*) You stupid bastard, Pratty. You stupid bastard.

Jack very slowly, miming his own agony, falls to the floor and lies still

The TABS *close very slowly as a Radio Announcer completes the news from the first curtain rise*

Announcer The police investigation into a missing man, a former Super-intendent at Scotland Yard, took a new turn today following the dis-covery of a dead body in the bricked-up cellar of a West Norwood house. As a result, it is understood that enquiries have been re-opened into the mysterious explosion at a Cornish tin mine last month when a so-far unidentified body was found in the wreckage.

CURTAIN

FURNITURE AND PROPERTY LIST

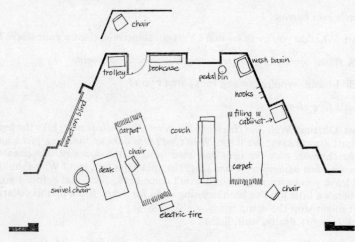

ACT I

SCENE 1

On stage: Desk. *On it:* Anglepoise lamp, telephone, glass of milk, memo pad, ashtray, carafe of water with glass, pen tray, folders, medical record cards, filing cards, prescription pad
Desk chair
Upright chair with Adcock's jacket over back. *In jacket pockets:* wallet, keys
Orthopaedic couch. *On it:* bloodstained sheet, pillow with blood-stained case, small bloodstained towel, wire hoop to support sheet over body's feet
Filing cabinet with various folders
Medical trolley with box of pills and other medicines
Bookcase with various medical books
Washbasin with warm water in it. *Over it:* Ascot water heater, paper towel roll in holder, electric clock (practical) set at 6.30
Hooks. *On them:* Adcock's anorak

Bentwood chair
On floor: Adcock's holdall with sweater, gym-shoes, dressing
On walls: various pictures, notices, posters, etc.
Outside door: chair
Carpets

Personal:　**Pratt:** wristwatch, packet of Rennies
Jack: wristwatch, rings

SCENE 2

Strike:　Body's foot hoop

Set:　Bloodstained sheet with two corners together
Clock at 7.15

Off stage:　Suitcase with sports shirt in laundry wrapper, clean pillow-case,
clean sheet, plastic bag of cotton-wool balls, empty plastic bag,
dustpan and brush, shaving mirror, nail scissors, nail file,
after-shave lotion, surgical spirit, comb **(Jack)**
Towel with two dabs of removing cream **(Jack)**
Bloodstained dinner jacket on hanger **(Jack)**
Bloodstained evening shirt **(Jack)**
Claw hammer **(Adcock)**

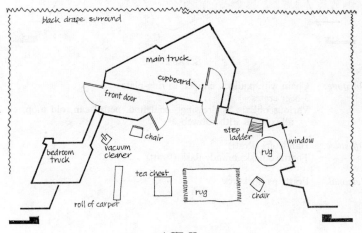

ACT II

SCENE 1

On stage:　Roll of carpet with Christine's overall draped over it
Tea-chest. *In it:* 2 glasses, scissors, duster, lampshades in tissue
paper, brush and comb in tissue paper, hand mirror in tissue paper
2 small chairs
Stepladder. *On it:* 2 curtains, box of curtain hooks
Vacuum cleaner

Pictures leaning against wall and other dressing
2 small carpets laid out on floor

Off stage: Bottle of champagne **(Jack)**
Parcel **(Christine)**
Gun **(Jack)**

Personal: **Christine:** handbag with door-key
Pratt: business cards, gun

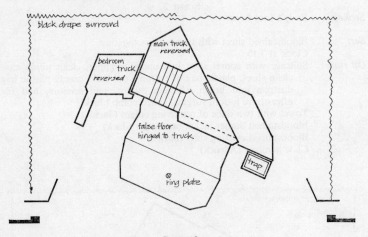

SCENE 2

On stage: Chain with padlock clipped to ring-plate
3 beer crates
Various objects as dressing—coal hod, petrol can, old mop, etc.,
all covered with cobweb

Off stage: Handcuffs **(Pratt)**
Thermos flask, brandy flask **(Pratt)**

Personal: **Pratt:** padlock key

LIGHTING PLOT

Property fittings required: ACT I—Angleposie lamp, electric clock, hanging
   lamp (over couch); ACT II, SCENE 1—Pendant; SCENE 2—bare hanging bulb
Interiors. A surgery. A living-room. A cellar

ACT I, SCENE 1
To open: All interior lighting on
Cue 1   **Adcock** returns after car drives away   (Page 12)
            Snap off back room light

ACT I, SCENE 2
To open: As close of previous scene
No cues

ACT II, SCENE 1. Afternoon
To open: Effect of late afternoon light
Cue 2   **Christine:** ". . . want to smirch it."   (Page 36)
            Start slow fade to dusk

ACT II, SCENE 2
To open: Very faint overall lighting
Cue 3   After CURTAIN rises   (Page 41)
            Bring up lighting very slowly to dim, with concentration on C stage
Cue 4   **Pratt** switches on light   (Page 42)
            Snap on single bulb and covering spot
Cue 5   **Pratt** switches off light   (Page 50)
            Revert to Cue 3 lighting
Cue 6   **Pratt** switches on light   (Page 50)
            Revert to Cue 4 lighting
Cue 7   **Pratt** switches off light   (Page 55)
            Revert to Cue 3 lighting
Cue 8   **Pratt** exits   (Page 55)
            Start slow fade till CURTAIN

EFFECTS PLOT

ACT I

SCENE 1

Cue 1	**Adcock** washes his hands	(Page 1)
	Sound of car driving up and stopping, car door slamming	
Cue 2	**Adcock** dries hands	(Page 1)
	Doorbell rings	
Cue 3	After **Pratt** and Adcock exit	(Page 12)
	Sound of car starting up and driving away	

SCENE 2

No cues

ACT II

SCENE 1

Cue 4	**Christine** turns from window	(Page 26)
	Sound of train passing	
Cue 5	**Christine:** "*What!?*"	(Page 28)
	Sound of train passing	
Cue 6	**Christine:** "Oh, Jack . . ."	(Page 29)
	Doorbell rings	
Cue 7	**Jack:** "Oh my Gawd!"	(Page 29)
	Doorbell rings	
Cue 8	**Jack:** "I keep getting distracted."	(Page 41)
	Champagne cork pops	

SCENE 2

Cue 9	**Pratt** lifts trap	(Page 51)
	Sound of running water	